Sales Mastery Series

Tough Love for *Easy Selling*

Gary A. Boye

The Dutch Uncle of Modern Selling invites you to "fire your inner novice!"

Published by Mastery Series Prints & Publishing

Copyright © 2014 by Gary A. Boye

All rights reserved. No part of this publication may be reproduced, distributed, or transmitted in any form or by any means, including photocopying, recording, or other electronic or mechanical methods, without the prior written permission of the publisher, except in the case of brief quotations embodied in critical reviews and certain other noncommercial uses permitted by copyright law. For permission requests, write to the publisher, addressed "Attention: Permissions Coordinator," at the address below.

ISBN-13: 978-1494913212

Gary A. Boye
Mastery Series Prints and Publishing
30 Brookdale Drive
Williamsville, NY 14221
garyboye3@gmail.com
716-799-5655

DEDICATION

To the men and women in sales
who choose to take their craft seriously

To their competitive spirit,
passion, and sense of awareness

To my inner critic who
got the hell out of my way

CONTENTS

Chapter		Page
	Introduction	IX
	Author's Note	XIII
1	Taught to Fail	1
2	Strictly Vanilla	7
3	In Blinking Lights	13
4	Fire Your Inner Novice	17
5	Learning to Learn	23
6	Let's Go Find Someone to Sell to	27
7	The Conversation	37
8	Somewhere Between Hello and Yes	43
9	Making a Proposal a Proposition	63
10	Should We "Always be Closing?"	69
11	Putting Things in Place	73
12	Scripts	77
13	Do They Really Think it Over?	85
14	Following Through	89
15	Yes, We Need to Know	93
16	An Axe to Grind	95
17	Getting Feedback Continuously	101
18	A Very Important Person	105
19	Working With Triplicates	109
20	The Artists Aren't Starving	113
	Epilogue	119
	Appendix	121
	About the Author	129

INTRODUCTION

WHEN A FRIEND found out I was writing a book as part of a series, he asked me what the series was about. I said it was about selling. Then he asked, "What about selling?" I said, "It's about competing in sales. The message behind the entire series is that if you're going to beat the competition, you've got to do things better than the competition." My friend then suggested, "Why don't you put that right in the beginning of the book?" And so I did, and there it is.

I'm beginning to believe there are enough "how to" guides on just about any subject to rival the number of grains of sand on a beach. It's not my intention to offer a step-by-step set of instructions about how to sell. I'm inclined to share stories and observations as illustrations of what successful selling really looks like. There are best practices within these chats which I hope my readers will find enticing and meaningful. Personally, I've read enough books to know readers like to skip around and that lets us both off the hook regarding pure sequence.

It was a humbling experience for me when I gave up the belief that levels of understanding were hierarchical. In

INTRODUCTION

truth, they exist laterally. All seven billion of us have different maps of reality. One person thinks she knows more about something than another, and, perhaps she does. Perhaps she doesn't. But it's her map and it reflects how she views the world around her. Real growth, for you, for me, for everyone, consists of expanding our maps. That doesn't mean we have to abandon our perch. I'm convinced that the smartest people in the world are the ones who know what they don't know. They are nurtured and sustained by their curiosity.

I wrote the first book in this series, *Sell or Get off the Pot*, with an attitude. It was a silly title for any book and it revealed my susceptibility to the desire to be clever at the price of caution in how I choose my words. I try to be much more careful today. In the preface, I voiced my concern for the "mythology and parrot platitudes that make up a lot of generic sales training." Throughout its pages, I mostly refrained from offering advice on tactics and techniques. I preferred to give real life examples of methodologies that were used by men and women who have achieved authentic and meaningful success in their sales careers. Mostly, I emphasized the importance of understanding the essence and nature of our practice. I referred often to The Four Applied Understandings that determine our success in selling. I asked the reader to accept that concept as gospel, even if it meant burying some common notions about selling that they had been fed. I have referenced those understandings again in this book as a way of disclosing my core beliefs. You will find that I also included them in the appendix.

In the preface of that earlier project, it's apparent that my words painted a rather grim picture of what has passed for sales education. I admit I had a real concern for being looked upon as contrarian. I don't like the stigma attached to contrarian beliefs. Too many people fake them to attract attention. I'm not wrapped in a self-image where I want to do that. But, I couldn't help but think that the world has enough books with a fictional world of selling between the covers. So I took solace. And, I remembered that I had discussed my intentions and viewpoints, along with how I would present them, with a few keen sales minds, and more than a few high achievers. They disagreed with nothing I would write. My concern dissolved.

I have often been bored with discussions on the "science vs. art debate" as it defines selling. I have never heard or read a conclusive argument that selling is a science. Art? Science and art do not exist on the same contextual plane. Selling is a practice and some people certainly practice it in an artful manner. I do and I want to disclose that upfront.

The best practitioners in sales have the ability to recognize certain patterns in behavior and circumstances they encounter. Art and science be damned, that particular trait sometimes can make it a game. Perhaps, that may account for the many sports analogies that pop up in sales lore. I have noticed that, much to their credit, most people with those abilities rarely allow themselves to let recognizable patterns trap them into assumptions. They haven't forgotten that no two situations are exactly alike.

One of the best things that ever happened to the sales profession is when women took their rightful place among some of the best. I always felt that they brought intangibles that somehow have raised the bar for excellence. The material in here is certainly not gender specific. You will find that I alternate masculine and feminine pronouns. I do this to give equal representation without encumbering the

INTRODUCTION

reading flow.

Certainly there are many best practices in selling. Several are included in this book along with the thoughts behind them. Those that I chose for inclusion are those that I believe are powerful. They are, nonetheless, a mixed bag. Some are subtle and some are highly innovative. Others are just plain common sense which is something I would never ask anyone to suspend.

Learn them. Adopt them. Renew them. Make them your very own. Most important--expand your own map.

I appreciate you.

AUTHOR'S NOTE

THERE ARE A FEW passages in this book that have appeared elsewhere. For instance, I repeated a sliver or two from my first book in The Sales Mastery Series, *Sell or Get off the Pot*, in a chapter devoted to prospecting. Also, while nobody was looking, I swiped a few words from two manuscripts that will morph into books for this series. One is called *20 Best Practices for Selling* and the other effort is currently in search of a title. Here, in Chapter 20, I repeated some of the text of a chapter in the first book. In it, I tried to deliver a message that I hope would be my legacy if I took myself more seriously. I did this, not because I have run out of things to say, but because I have loads of reasons to reinforce the thoughts I share with the reader.

In other words, my intentions are good.

-- Gary

ONE
Taught to Fail

SOME THINGS LEAVE a lasting impression. I got my first taste of fictional sales training in a room filled with twenty two other bodies that were engaged in selling life insurance policies. I was twenty three years old at the time. I was eager, hungry, and filled with the promises of glossy brochures that the company handed out to recruits, all depicting a storybook life for those among us who "got going when the going got tough."

We sat and watched a 16 millimeter training film that featured a third rate character actor portraying a bumbling salesman who was learning to "ask for the order." At one point the script in that situation comedy even had him saying, "May I have your order please?"

At the Friday morning meetings we were taught a lot of clichés. One of them was "Always be closing." It was called The ABC of Selling. Another was "Assume the sale." We were told that selling is a numbers game. We were asked to memorize rebuttals to common objections because selling is all about overcoming objections. Our managers reminded us that we would not make it if we couldn't "close." They instructed us never to ask a question that could be answered with a "no."

One of the things I remember vividly was that we were expected to believe that the relationship between buyer and seller is a win-lose proposition. We were told the following: "When you ask a closing question, shut up! The first person to talk loses." To emphasize, they actually shouted "Shut up!"

Most of what we were taught had little resemblance to how people actually behave with one another. Even at age twenty three, I knew that. However, that was the only type of guidance I was getting from the company.

To put it bluntly, we were taught to fail.

That was my introduction to sales training. It took place over forty years ago.

These pages are about the craft of the superior salesperson. I was inspired to write them by three factors in my life. The first I can reveal in the form of a confession. I am somewhat angered by much of what still passes itself off as sales education. A lot of it resembles the same tired material I described above.

Sadly, there are few bricks and mortar schools of selling. Colleges and universities have somehow managed to avoid adding sales courses to their curriculums. That rankles me. I know that our culture's economy is largely driven by the movement of products and services. Of course, the Internet has afforded an opportunity for self appointed experts to attempt to ply their trade of teaching others how things are sold. Articles and blogs abound with tips, clichés, rules, bullet points, secrets, laws, and motivational affirmations. Mostly, we are offered survival tools for an imaginary world of selling.

My second enticement was a gnawing sensation that I could distract a few people from the mythology and parrot platitudes that make up a lot of generic sales training. I felt that I could provide a meaningful roadmap to lead them on a path of productivity and financial reward.

It has been many years since I decided to "fire my inner novice." That's an expression I invented when I learned that people get good at things out of choice followed by commitment. I believe that almost anything can be mastered through awareness, understanding, and practice. Too many people think mastery is for the other guy.

The third and deciding factor in my decision to write this book was that I have people in my life who are there to encourage me because they share my frustrations with the status quo and my passion for the art of selling.

Once we take our craft seriously, we don't have to think long and hard before realizing that the "profession" is a tight group, surrounded by a majority of amateurs who need to learn how to sell, but first need to learn how to learn. The underachievers continue to seek survival tools, while those that make the big money are doing much more than surviving because they truly are the fittest. They shine before their markets, and the competition makes them seem so much brighter. Within these pages I want to share not only a vital basis of understanding for our topic, but also a formula for learning.

The lure of a career in sales has always seemed attached to a promise. Typically, the promise sounds something like this: "If you do this, this, and that, you can make big money in sales." Sometimes the words, "All you have to do" are plugged in. Does that sound familiar? Well, I like simplicity as much as the next fellow but an awful lot depends on just what, exactly, others would have us do. I want to keep it simple and when we explore the pretext of this work which says that success in selling is found in four things and only four things, it is so simple it is profound. Of course, many simple things are profound, and maybe that's why their lessons often escape us.

A lot of salespeople, who are seeking to improve their lot, come looking for techniques and tactics. Some come hoping for magic. Others want to map out a strategy to reach their objectives. But we can't get very far in sales without both awareness and understanding. The tactics, magic, and strategy take on new life when they are filtered through an understanding of the "why" of what we are doing. Achieving the financial rewards in sales is about embracing and applying four understandings, all of which continuously unfold in the following pages. They are ingrained in every topic we will discuss. As a matter of fact, if we make a habit of relating everything we practice in selling to one or more of those four understandings, we will find ourselves on the right path. That path is not crowded and those individuals who work in a highly competitive environment can take heart in that fact.

Within the scope of my own limitations which includes a tendency to invent an occasional term, I try to use the plain language we might converse with over a cup of coffee. What I have to say comes from my experience, my observations, my success in selling, and the hard lessons I took to heart. My words are driven by a mighty motivation to get my message across. In the past, as well as the present, I managed to get my message across to many thousands of people who became my clients. Mostly, not always, I used plain language with them also.

I began these pages with a confession. I have another which bears explanation. I'm writing this book for leaders. I truly harbor a desire for significance as much as the next person and the best contribution I can make lies in reaching those leaders that can help and influence others. One of the things I discovered over the last forty years is that the superior salesperson has something in common with the superior sales organization. Most high earners have somehow managed to create their own infrastructure. They choose to remain in control of their own destiny. I have noticed that great sales organizations are founded on core principles and beliefs that extend from the top down. Their leaders actually enforce alignment with the company philosophy. As the saying goes, it's their football. It is not surprising that some of the best sales training in the world is shaped from within those organizations. Those men and women in charge never lose sight of the vested interest the company has in the performance level of the sales force. It's my hope that my contribution will deliver keen observations, insight, and a philosophy that can sustain huge profits for both the individual and the organization.

I welcome you to a world of real people, real situations, and real selling.

TWO
Strictly Vanilla

I'M A STORYTELLER and I have a couple of stories from my past that I want to share. One actually has a story within a story.

Long before blogging became a household word, I expressed some strong opinions on an open Internet sales forum where so-called experts had convened in the hope of getting noticed. A few days later, I had my ego stroked when a woman called me and introduced herself as the editor of an extremely popular subscription journal on selling. She said she liked the way I articulated my thoughts. She was wondering if I was interested in writing a few articles for her publication. What they were willing to pay me was more than generous, and I agreed to do it.

One of the first articles she asked me to write was on "How to Deal with Tough Customers." It seemed to me that it was an easy topic to write about. Over my career in sales I had faced some real hard noses. Truth be told, I always fancied myself pretty good at striking a harmonic chord with badasses. Before I go further and so that my story has more impact, I'll reveal my secret. I make it a habit to appeal to a person's "better nature." I try hard to do right for my client and I don't want them tripping over their own feet.

Of course, the publication had rules for their articles. One of them was that you couldn't write in the first person. Also, you couldn't write as if you were addressing the second person. In other words, you couldn't say "I" or "you" or any other first or second person pronouns. (Thank goodness I make my own rules here!)

I wrote the article as I do with most of what I write. I draw from my own experiences, good, bad, but never indifferent. However, I could not refer to myself if I chose to provide a real-life example. This was tough; I'm a serial storyteller. Someone else had to play my part. Just imagine if they made a movie from it!

I'm not fond of bullet point lists, so, rest assured, they were not going to get *Twelve Ways to Deal with Tough Customers* from yours truly. I stayed glued to my core belief on the issue which is all about appealing to a person's better nature. I illustrated with a story from my own experience and kept it in line with a third person narrative.

My example went something like this. It seems on a very busy Saturday afternoon in one of a retail chain's floor covering showrooms, a young salesman was being "run over the coals" by a man who was intent on making someone sweat blood before he would agree to spending twelve hundred dollars for some carpet that his wife was drooling over. Testosterone was ruling his day and making the salesman's day one that he wished he had not shown up for. Well, it turned out that the CEO of the company happened to be visiting that location and was watching the situation, drawn to the young man's frustration. He decided to introduce himself to the man and his wife and ask if he could be of any help. At that moment, the young salesman was asked to take a telephone call from a customer. Meanwhile the man's wife had wandered over to another display. The man decided to turn up his level of obstinacy and display it to the CEO. You might say that this was his customary buying process. Finally, our CEO friend had listened to enough and said, "Will you cut out the crap? I'm trying to close a deal for this kid!"

What happened next was a complete turnaround for our tough guy buyer. His response, spoken in a soft apologetic tone, was, "Oh."

From that moment on, everyone was part of a team that was going to get the man's wife her carpet, and, help a young, inexperienced salesman.

Psychologists might infer that "transference" took place. For instance, maybe the couple had a son or daughter the same age as the salesman. Whatever, happened, we know that the buyer's attitude changed, revealing a "better" nature, and the willingness to help rather than hinder. It was a "shift" in the man's "frame" of mind.

A sale was made and like all gratifying stories, it had a happy ending. But that's only the story within the story. Let's get back to me, my article, and my generous editor. My work was published with all the good stuff about appealing to a person's better nature--with one catch. The illustrative example about the man, the CEO, the wife, and the young salesman was omitted. The publication wanted vanilla.

I suspect that stories about real people, complete with warts and out of the "ordinary" behavior, were as unwelcome as first person narratives. As a first person myself, I couldn't be in the story even though I'm real and don't have to pinch myself to prove it.

STRICTLY VANILLA

I promise you that within the qualities and limitations inherent in how I express myself, I write these pages drawing only from the real world that I have known. It would be nice if we could jump into one of those glossy brochures or training films that depict selling like Currier and Ives depicts icy roads. But, personally, I'm not that photogenic.

That brings me to my second story.

A few years ago, a woman friend invited me to attend a class on labor management that she was taking at a local university. It sounded like something that would interest me and I went with her in the capacity of a visitor/observer with the instructor's kind permission. This was the first session of the course and its purpose was to give an introduction and outline of the various topics that would be discussed. Toward the end of the allotted time, the instructor asked if anyone had any questions. He then acknowledged a young man who had immediately raised his hand. The student's question could be construed as somewhat provocative. He said, "Inasmuch as you're are going to be teaching a course on labor management, it's only fair that you tell us where you stand. Where is your bias? Who do you lean towards--labor or management? In other words, are you pro-labor or pro-management?"

The instructor didn't miss a beat. I recall his exact words, He said, "I'm neither. I'm pro-situation. If you're really asking for my background, I'll tell you. I'm an ironworker."

Why has that simple brief exchange stuck with me all these years? Maybe it has to do with some wisdom my father shared when I was a boy. He said, "Always consider the source." Maybe it was because the instructor's answer would cover a lot of preconceptions among the attendees in that class. His answer implied a personal belief that it's important to consider every situation on its own merit.

We must consider the source of our information. I'm the source of what you are now reading in the hope of discerning and expanding views on selling for a living. I owe it to the reader to tell some things about myself. The first thing I want to tell is that I have a philosophy of sales and it permeates my writing and coaching. Over and above everything that follows, I believe we should express what we believe.

My philosophy of sales includes a core belief that we are always being compared. Our clients and prospects are comparing the experience they have with us to the experiences they have with others. Our success in selling largely depends on making the other experiences pale by comparison.

I believe and I teach that preparedness is the most important skill in selling. It is that skill that facilitates and magnifies all of the other things that we have learned to do right. I believe that honest enlightened questions are critical for the sales engagement. Further, I recognize "closing sales" as a progression of consent--not an event as is popularly taught.

I would never be as foolish as to attempt to write an all-inclusive treatise on the subject of selling. Opportunities abound in too many flavors and nothing can be described as "all relevant" more than the flighty thing we sometimes call success. To paraphrase a favorite author, Stephen Covey, I have sought to understand, and then to be understood. I believe that without those words, I would not have the audacity to write this stuff.

THREE
In Blinking Lights

ONE DAY I had a conversation with that Little Voice in My Head. It took place halfway through the gathering of material for these pages which advises that there are Four Things that determine our success in selling.

"You can't say 'things,'" the Little Voice said. "Call them 'secrets', or 'laws', or 'rules.'"

"They are none of those," I argued. "They are 'teachings'. Nobody made them a law or a rule. And they are nobody's secret. They are what four decades of lessons and accomplishments in sales taught me. Every single success story I observed in myself and others validates those teachings. I take no credit for inventing some kind of magic formula."

We bantered back and forth and I almost won the argument with The Little Voice—until something occurred to me. It had to do with the words of author and educator Stephen Covey, whose classic book, *The Seven Habits of Highly Effective People*, remains one of the very best treatises on personal development. Covey said, *"Seek first to understand, then to be understood."*

My four things were not just things, they were understandings. Actually, they are meant to be applied understandings. They are not just factors in the science, art, practice, business, game (pick one) of selling. They are the determinants.

Voila!

I'm hell bent to influence the reader with my core belief regarding what it takes to succeed in sales. Here then is what I observed, utilized, and teach as the Four Applied Understandings that determine our success in selling:

1. We are being compared. Every potential customer we meet is comparing the experience they have with us to the experiences they have with others. Our success in selling largely depends on making the other experiences pale by comparison.

2. Honest insightful questions are the building blocks of a sale.

3. Preparedness is the most important skill in selling.

4. Closing is a progression of consent.

It would be wonderful if we could carry those words in blinking lights on the inside of our foreheads. However, here's a suggestion: It might pay to write them on a three by five card and carry them with you, at least until the time we retire from selling, managing a sales force, or being a CEO or chairman in a company driven by sales.

I use words like "factors and "determinants", but there

is a clear difference between the two. My dictionary tells me that when I "determine", I settle or decide conclusively. I ascertain or conclude, after observation or consideration. (In all fairness, I admit that I have chosen and paraphrased the definitions which conform to this discussion.) On the other hand, "factor" is defined as an element or cause that contributes to a result.

There are Two Programs Running

In *Twice as Good as 2nd Best*™, a course for professionals who sell, we introduced the concept, *Simul-Selling*™. Although we don't pretend to be neurologists or psychologists, we know that there are two programs running simultaneously in almost all buyer-seller conversations. To put it simply, a prospective buyer evaluates the product, offer, and proposition while, at the same time, also evaluates the experience with the salesperson. On the seller side of the table, a skilled practitioner is aware that she is really making two presentations: her product/offer, and herself. I'll throw in the common and fluffy over-simplification to further support the point: "Before you can sell your product, you have to sell yourself." Let's be totally honest; the factors that can influence a sale probably border on infinite and only a few are within our control. Our job is not to lose a sale by our own hand. I cover some common factors in these pages. We'll also pay attention to those things that will lose a sale before we can bat an eye. The game changer is that we're going to filter factors through the lens of the determinants—namely The Four Applied Understandings that cause our success.

The late author and motivational speaker Jim Rohn hit

the mark when he said, "Success is neither magical nor mysterious. Success is the natural consequence of consistently applying the basic fundamentals." Having awareness of what takes place between buyer and seller is fundamental if we are going to be good at what we do. Understanding the dynamics involved is even more important.

Mark Twain once wrote, "People will buy from people they know, like, and trust." In his excellent book, *Endless Referrals*, networking and referral expert Bob Burg used similar words. He said, "All things being equal, people do business with, and refer business to, people they know, like and trust."

We shouldn't ignore those "golden rules." They are huge factors in selling. Of course we do often buy from people we have not known from prior experiences. Also, it's a safe bet that people sometimes buy from people they don't particularly like. On occasion, it can be expedient to do so. But those are exceptions and we must not toss aside good advice because of exceptions.

Confidence, the trust factor, is huge. Conditions of mutual trust and respect between buyer and seller are something we should aim for and seek to identify always.

I know that the so-called psychology of selling always has appeal. It has significance, so long as the focus is on how people behave rather than reasons why they behave that way. We can leave that to the psychologists who have their own trouble trying to agree with one another. After all, you and I have stuff to sell. Without being Svengalis, the battle for the mind of the buyer can be won.

Our rewards will directly align with willingness to internalize and appreciate those Applied Understandings.

Blinking lights, remember?

FOUR
Fire Your Inner Novice

WE MAY HAVE met before. In *Sell or Get off the Pot*, I titled a chapter, *Navigating the Seas of Buyer Resistance*. The topic is so important that I have repeated it in this book. I describe buyer resistance as the core challenge we face in selling. It doesn't matter what level of expertise we currently enjoy. Buyer resistance is there for the novice and for the master alike. It is part of the environment we work in. If the challenge was no longer there, the practice of selling would be relegated to the mundane tasks of facilitation. For some, it would take the fun out of it. The quality of performance in any endeavor is always measured by how we transcend its greatest challenge.

Cheer up! Buyer resistance isn't going to take a hike any time soon.

"Can't" is a Cluster of "Won'ts."

I coach people to make a habit of expressing what they believe. Not everybody has an easy time with that. A lot of people will express with apparent passion merely what they've heard from others. The dogma that exists in so-called sales education is filled with cliché's that people rarely take the time to discern properly. Once again, I have an obligation to practice what I preach. The title of this series is *Sales Mastery Series*. I believe mastery in anything is a journey, not a destination. I know that a novice can start that journey with a single step. When that happens, everything changes. But most people don't take that step. That's because many of us face another core challenge, novices and masters alike. It consists of the resistance we face from within.

Several years ago, I read a book by A. L. Williams, a man who founded a huge direct sales insurance company. He was an inspiration to many who modeled his thinking. He expressed something that I wrote down and always carried with me. He said, *"All you can do is all you can do, but all you can do is enough."* I have wondered about the first time that thought ever came to Williams' mind. Was it his own first step that took him onto the highway of mastery? I would be hard-pressed to believe that he was born and raised with the luxury of not having to face the inner resistance everyone else faces.

Too many people think mastery is for the other guy. I love the words of the great martial artist, Bruce Lee. He said, *"If you want to learn to swim, jump into the water. On dry land no frame of mind is ever going to help you."* He also said, *"Don't fear failure. Not failure, but low aim, is the crime. In great attempts it is glorious even to fail."*

Is fear at the heart of why people remain at the status quo? Are we intimidated? Or--do the words of David J. Schwartz, author of the classic, *The Magic of Thinking Big*, ring true when he pointed out that mediocrity can be socially acceptable? Yes--I think we should take time to ponder on that one.

Many salespeople place arbitrary limits on their own progress, denying themselves the types of goals that lead to consistent improvement because they are stuck in a perpetual state of "can't."

I took up sailing later in life than most people. It brings much joy to my world. It also brings pride. I'm proud because I was very intimidated by the sport. I took the plunge and I learned sailing and learned it well. I became a respected member of the sailing community where I live. I had never thought those people would accept me, but they do. They respect my passion as well as the skills I have acquired. I learn every time I'm on the water. I learn from others. But--most of all I learn from inside myself because I crowded out that inner novice whose favorite advice is, "You can't." I love to sail my sailboat. What a feeling being one with the wind and water with nothing but the faint hum of weather helm on my tiller. So beautiful. When I think about sailing, I think about those things. I could also, if I choose, think about heavy weather, knockdowns, capsizing, and mildew for that matter. All part of it and I can handle it. They call it forehandedness, and I'm prepared for those things. But I keep my mind in the right place and I keep my inner novice at bay.

Yes--it takes one step to get on the road to mastery--a road with no destination but huge fulfillment. There are no intermediates in selling. "Intermediate" is a word that describes a practiced novice. It's not a good place to be in our journey. If we haven't already done so, we'll fire that inner novice. It's not our friend. We can become extraordinary. It's a choice we make.

Can We Predict Sales Success by Assessing an Individual's Personality?

We've heard that question and I think the answer is that we can, but the reliability of that prediction can be suspect. Who is doing the assessing and what arbitrary measure of personality are they using? We hear talk about introverts and extroverts and their respective odds on making it as salespeople. It was the great psychologist Carl Jung who introduced the concept of introvert and it had little to do with shyness. I doubt "nerd" was in his vocabulary. Jung saw introverts as those people who relied on getting their feedback from within. He also observed that most people had both introvert and extrovert tendencies. What I'm saying is that there are popular and less reliable use of such words and distinctions--similar to the popular misuse of the term, inferiority complex, which has little to do with the meaning of "complex" in psychology. Man is a complex creature, and predictability has never completely caught up with that complexity. But we can and do observe.

What Does Excellence Look Like?

In the open forum days of SalesPractice.com, we observed the attitudes, dispositions, and apparent reasoning of thousands of sales practitioners from a wide range of industries. Some were newcomers to their field. Many had been in sales for decades. Based on those studies, we were able to construct a matrix that differentiated the apparent mindsets of the average and the extraordinary in sales. If we want to model excellence, it pays to know what excellence looks like. The following chart illustrates critical attitudes and beliefs that our observations revealed:

Mindsets: A Comparison Chart

The Average	The Extraordinary
I have to get better at what I'm doing.	I seek to understand the nature of what I'm doing.
I have to achieve.	I accomplish.
I have to prepare for the unexpected.	I prepare for the expected.
I have to react.	I create.
I'm thinking too small. I have to think big.	I see the big picture. I do the little things that matter.
I will assume the sale.	I will intend the sale
I want the buyer to make a favorable decision.	I want the buyer to justify a favorable decision.
I see selling as a game of persuasion.	I see selling as a practice of influence and facilitation.
I need to make contacts. I want to build rapport.	I want to enter the lives of others. I seek conditions of mutual trust and respect.
I know how to sell.	I know why people buy.
I'll settle for making a good living.	I'll settle for taking my place among the top money earners.

At first glance, the differences might seem subtle. It's my hope that as we continue to explore the nature of our art, the disparity of mindsets between the common and the extraordinary will become increasingly clear. I invite the reader to refer to this chart often as we move along in these studies. If we are serious about our craft, there is only one place to see ourselves. You and I are engaging in these pages because we are indeed curious and serious. We're not chained to a fixed mindset. Instead, we have a growth mindset. We belong among the extraordinary

In the next chapter, we're going to discuss in detail what the differences are between those two mindsets and how they occur from the way we learn.

FIVE
Learning to Learn

SALES NOVICES REMAIN stuck at that stage way too often. I have seen many of them attempt to compensate for their lack of knowledge in ways that hold them back. They want to reinvent. The believe that they can find a better way than the system that has been laid out for them. In fairness, sometimes it works for them. However, for many, the opportunities to learn their craft become platforms for auditions. They want to perform with little regard for learning. As a result, they showcase their limitations. Perhaps they came from an environment where they enjoyed some self-perceived status as "head-of-the class." They do not, as the Zen saying goes, "empty their minds."

These practiced novices fall into the category of "entity learners." I'll share a story about how I learned that term.

A few years ago, a movie came out called *Searching for Bobby Fischer*. It had little to do with the famous and infamous grandmaster of chess referred to in the title. The movie was based on a book of the same name. It told the story of a gifted child, Josh Waitzkin, and was written by his father. Young Josh had an aptitude for chess, and became one of the country's top players as a boy. His learning process, as well as his parent's challenges in having a gifted child, are depicted in the book and dramatized in the film.

Years have passed since the movie was made. Since then, Josh as an adult wrote a marvelous book called *The Art of Learning*. In it, he reveals something I find astounding. This same man, who was a child prodigy in chess, became a world champion of martial arts!

His gifts were not about chess or martial arts. He had the ability to learn. To put it more succinctly, Josh has, and shares with us, a superior way to learn. He had conducted research on a certain theory of intelligence and learning, which categorizes people as either entity learners or incremental learners. In brief, entity learners see their skill or intelligence level at a given task as a fixed entity (as in, "I'm good at math" or "I'm an excellent swimmer"). In many cases, proud parents, or people in their immediate circle, overindulge in reinforcing the perception of the person's ability. As a result they tend to stay at the same level and often overestimate it.

Incremental learners tend to attribute their successes or failures at tasks to their amount of effort or work, truly believing they can master anything with enough energy put in. They live with curiosity. They want to learn more. And they know what they don't know. Psychologists call this a growth mindset. Carol Dweck, a renowned professor of psychology at Stanford University, has expounded on this. Her 2006 book, *Mindset, The New Psychology of Success*, is one I highly recommend to people who want to learn how to learn. She teaches that the growth mindset will allow a person to live a less stressful and more successful life. You can see the similarities to what Waitzkin provided us in

Dweck's definition of fixed and growth mindsets from a 2012 interview:

> *"In a fixed mindset, students believe their basic abilities, their intelligence, their talents, are just fixed traits. They have a certain amount and that's that, and then their goal becomes to look smart all the time and never look dumb. In a growth mindset students understand that their talents and abilities can be developed through effort, good teaching and persistence. They don't necessarily think everyone's the same or anyone can be Einstein, but they believe everyone can get smarter if they work at it."*

Entity learners, those with a fixed mindset, seldom take risks, and they often get emotionally crushed by any type of defeat. Incremental learners are ready to accept a challenge they may not succeed at, and don't take defeat as failure. They push themselves, and often enjoy life fuller.

Very few chess players or martial artists are self taught. Very few superstars in any field of endeavor are self taught. Waitzkin learned chess because he exposed himself to masters and was taught how to learn. Men like Bruce Lee and Chuck Norris shared their knowledge in martial arts with one another and among many masters. In our profession of selling, the great sales educator and expert on motivation, Tom Hopkins, learned from J. Douglas Edwards, his forerunner who he called "The Father of Modern Selling."

The choice will always be ours. Will we permit ourselves to be chained to what we think we already know, or, will we allow our growth to simply happen by remaining open, curious, and aware?

I believe, with that question, I have made the obvious compelling.

SIX
Let's Go Find Someone to Sell to

TYPICALLY, A PERSON takes a new sales job and the honeymoon ends at about the same time that he is handed his first task. "Here–you need to prospect for customers." After that, it would all depend on the particular industry for us to assess and address the survival rate. Here's a glimpse of those men and women who stay on the journey and survive very well.

First stage: Clueless

Second stage: Influenced by someone who says, "It's all about "finding."

Enlightened stage: Influenced by one's own mind that says, "It's all about "connecting."

They call it prospecting for a reason. I still like the image of the old miner on the creek's shore mining for gold. It reinforces the right perspective--that prospecting boils down to "finding" people who will listen to our story. As a matter of fact, isn't that what marketing is all about?

Now there's a word: "marketing." Such a vague term! We all seem to define it differently if we define it at all. Different perspectives vary even among those individuals who are advanced in business or who teach classes on the subject. Let's look at the official definition put forth by The American Marketing Association:

> *Marketing is the activity, set of institutions, and processes for creating, communicating, delivering, and exchanging offerings that have value for customers, clients, partners, and society at large. (Approved October 2007)*

Yikes! Okay--that helps. Now we know what the ten bazillion self-described "marketing consultants" do to make ends meet.

The late renowned advertising genius, David Ogilvy, defined marketing simply as "objectivity". Those who teach strategy define it as a battle for the mind of the consumer. I can think of three giants of advertising who agreed with the notion that advertising itself was "salesmanship." If the goal of advertising was not to sell, then the efforts would have very little value. I'm intellectualizing here and intellectualizing does not make sales. Someone much wiser than myself told me if you want to find meaning, don't look to semantics. Regardless of how the lines are drawn, the question remains, "To what end?" Prospecting consists of finding and connecting with prospective buyers. You will get no argument from me if you want to put it into the marketing column. Companies can use direct response marketing venues such as radio, newspapers, television, flyers, billboards, or the Internet. They can devise direct mail campaigns, promote attendance at networking breakfasts, create referral programs, or set up trade show exhibits. Or, they can have their people knock on doors.

Even the Most Complex Sale Starts with Hello.

Lately we seem to be inundated with a lot of sales morticians intent on giving "cold calling" a premature burial. I've had more than one occasion to dispute the Cold Calling is Dead Theory. Recently I was asked to share some sort of "gem" which I took to mean a tactic, maneuver, technique, or a secret sauce recipe, to make the cold calling concept more appealing.

I don't share "gems" as readily as I attempt to share understanding. "Cold calling" has one overriding stigma-- that of intrusiveness. Most salespeople might not use that word, but the fact remains that most of us don't want to suffer the discomfort of being perceived as intrusive. We can evoke the tired phrase, "fear of rejection", if you like. On this topic, the following six words have more value than all of the guru's books, blogs, and, webinars combined.

- **Make the calls.**
- **Tell the truth.**

In sales we talk to people. Some we know. Some we don't know. Nothing unusual about that. There has never been a need to package that activity into a term (cold calling), and present it as some horrendously frightening activity like it's going to show up on Halloween and say "Boo!"

For over a century there have been salespeople who are very effective in dropping in on merchants who weren't expecting them aka the cold call. At the same time, there have been those who were clueless on how to do it effectively. Both groups still exist. I know a woman who is the highest earning media advertising salesperson in her area. Rita, who we will discuss further, does all of her prospecting in the effective manner I just described. She has worked that way for over twenty years. She continues to grow in earnings and client acquisition. As the saying goes, she "will not fix what ain't broke."

It's in knowing how.

Meeting new people, introducing ourselves, making ours, and our company's presence felt, are good things, aren't they? One has to go back to the concept of the purposeful call. Rita has one--and only one--purpose for her initial contact. It is to briefly introduce herself to the decision maker and ask for consent to a later non-decision making interview in which she could explain more about what her company provides, and, learn more about the marketing objectives of the merchant.

Cold calling does not deserve the bad rap that some so-called experts would have us accept. In sales discussions where tactics and techniques are evaluated, a lot of people are glued to "one call closing" scenarios. Twenty or thirty years ago, many industries depended on such sales strategies. There was a time when there was no Walmart to sell us our vacuum cleaner. There were no Internet sources to supplant thirty two volume leather bound reference libraries. Direct sales morphed largely into MLM, and even that became a more complex sale. Today, a greater percentage of salespeople are involved in more complex sales. But--the most complex sale still starts with hello.

Asking Permission

Regardless of how we attempt to initiate conversations with prospective buyers, nothing takes the place of finding ways to ask permission to do so. Over the last fifteen years, I have had hundreds of men and women, mostly newcomers to sales, ask my help in creating a "cold calling" script for them. In almost all those cases, there was no evidence of a worthy lead generation program in place at the companies they worked for. For those who had embarked on a self-employment journey, the feelings ranged from frustration, to cluelessness, to panic. Prepared scripts can have their place. In a later chapter we're going to examine that topic. I don't design generic scripts.

Lately, the concept of the "elevator speech" has become popular. Personal commercials! What can we say about ourselves to a stranger in an attempt to connect with a potential client? I've been asked to evaluate some of those, too. For most of them , I can say that if anybody tried to test one of those elevator speeches on me, I'd get off at the next floor and take the stairs.

Too many people have never learned, or forgotten, that the best way to connect is to talk about the other guy, not ourselves.

Scripts and elevator talks are part of a culture who believes selling is a numbers game. It is not. That's because, in effective practice, quality rules over quantity. The movers and shakers in selling are highly selective as to where they place their efforts. They carefully define their market of potential buyers. They focus their efforts on approaching individuals in that realm. When they make an initial contact, either by phone, in person, or by written correspondence, they ask permission to take the next step. The "progression of consent" formula starts at the very beginning and remains throughout.

Three Important Areas of Focus

I've observed that the big money earners spend less time measuring their success and more time projecting it. They identify their market. They identify the decision makers within that market. They periodically identify, in realistic fashion, their projected business for the short term. I'll add that they are very truthful to themselves in the process. To put it simply, they can pretty much tell you where their next sales are going to come from. If more sales organizations could adhere to the activity of realistic projecting, they could increase sales production dramatically.

To illustrate the prospecting progression, I want to present thumbnail sketches of three real-life individuals who enjoy remarkable success at finding and cultivating new clients. Let's take a moment to walk in the shoes of Rita, Harlan, and Catherine.

Having a Plan and Working it Religiously

Rita is an account manager for a major radio station in a large metropolitan area in the Midwest. Media advertising is highly competitive. In most areas, only the cream of the crop enjoys large incomes. Rita does because she outsells her competition on a regular basis.

Because of her radio station's listenership rankings, its advertising rates are substantially higher than most of Rita's competitors. Although she can offer a high return on investment, her prospects often initially balk because of perceived budget constraints. To use an old phrase, Rita has her work cut out for her.

She meets those challenges of resistance regularly and is able to build solid relationships with her clients. However, Rita has to find those prospects in order to tell her story. She has a plan for her work and she works it religiously. She prospects by making unannounced calls, in person, to businesses that she has carefully chosen as those that would benefit from the advertising she sells.

Rita has one, and only one, objective on that call. It is to meet, face-to-face, the person responsible for buying advertising and ask permission to return at an appointed time to discuss her station. She never gives a presentation at that first meeting. She calls it a "commitment objective." She has learned that her success in selling comes from taking small steps in a progression of consent.

A Dyed-in-the-Wool Target Marketer

At age twenty two, Harlan began his work as an insurance salesman with a company that specializes in using a financial planning approach. He had no experience and no college degree. He managed to be recruited "under the radar" because of a family friend employed by the company. The friend offered to take him under his wing. As is typical with insurance companies, he was asked to compile a large list of names that he could approach by cold calling over the phone. He was provided with a company prepared script and told not to stray from it. Harlan was assigned to "the bullpen" where he spent his days calling, seeking appointments, and facing the rejection one might expect. The work was wearing and emotionally draining and his managers acted like drill sergeants in a military boot camp. However, they were keen on the nature of the type of prospect the company wanted to pursue.

Harlan's mentors wanted him to talk to successful business owners--not executive types. He followed their instructions and learned something very useful which had a huge impact on his career and the extraordinary financial success he has enjoyed in the last two decades. He discovered that it was much easier to reach people at the top than it was to talk with management types. Moreover, the patriarchs and matriarchs of large businesses would take the time to listen to what he had to say. "I noticed a much different attitude among people at the top," he explains. "I believe that most of them have not forgotten their roots. They are receptive to new ideas. They don't think they 'know it all.' They seem willing to hear about ideas that could make their situation even better."

Working with the business owner market opened the door to the second stage of prospecting that built Harlan's success. Referrals were much easier to come by because his market's culture was one where referrals flowed with little resistance.

She Lives by Her Principles of Prospecting.

Catherine is a small business owner on the west coast of Florida who has nurtured the area's prominent restaurant and tourist industry with her marketing savvy. She created the Sarasota Sally phenomenon which grabbed a slice of tight restaurant advertising budgets while providing a return that the newspapers and other media had promised but rarely delivered.

Restaurant owners are a tough sell. They work long hours and have very limited attention spans for salespeople who need to tell their story. Just making an appointment can be the toughest sell of all.

Catherine lives by four principles in her prospecting efforts.

First, she seeks ways to be different. She wants to stand out from the crowd. Catherine believes that since everyone else is cold calling and canvassing prospects, traditional approaches will be the least effective and the most frustrating approach to take. She told us, "The last thing I want is to be one more salesperson walking through the door, just like the fifty who came before." Her first step, for instance is a mailing piece which attracts attention because of the small gift enclosed. The mailer also announces that she will be calling the recipient to ask for a brief, non-decision making appointment.

Second, she takes baby steps. She never asks too much from the prospect at any one juncture of the engagement. She believes he biggest mistake most people make in prospecting is that they try for too much in one step. In so doing, the prospect is turned off and they terminate the dialogue.

Third, Catherine goes for quality--not quantity. She carefully targets who she wants to talk to. She points out that when people talk about working the numbers, they think that more is always better. Her method includes choosing a smaller number of prospects, who are reasonably targeted, and putting some effort into nurturing them.

Last, she is patient and persistent, but she is never pushy. She doesn't try to skip steps in her prospecting method. Since she is never asking for too much in a single step, it's comfortable for her prospect and it's comfortable for her too.

As I write this chapter on prospecting, I have in mind that that some of the information and ideas could provide juicy material for a roundtable discussion among a group of serious and aspiring sales professionals. I'm hoping that some of my readers may see it in the same light. If I was sitting with that group, I would want to offer my two cents exactly as I'm doing here.

The real life examples from the experiences of Rita, Harlan, and Catherine have two obvious and dominant common threads. One is their commitment to persistence and endurance. The other is their discipline in staying with a consistent tested strategy. However, we can't view real life examples and slot them into Utopian world views.

At the first stage in his job as a life insurance salesman, Harlan was certainly working the numbers game. He probably didn't have much choice. In that specific arena of selling, the attrition rate is very high and he could have just as easily failed. But he didn't fail. When he happened on a couple of solid opportunities, he was able to parlay those connections into a stream of referrals that built a very successful career. My point is that when he entered the second stage of mining qualified prospects, he entered the realm that Rita works in, and that Catherine has perfected and describes as quality over quantity.

I believe what these three professionals have shared with us sends a strong message. It is this: Good sales strategies and methodologies are also highly effective time management systems. Incremental short term planning rules the day when it comes to achieving long term results.

SEVEN
The Conversation

I WONDER WHO came up with the term, "sales process." Over the years I've developed as much disdain for those words as a *fromager* would have for processed cheese. Frankly, I would cringe if I tried to conjure thoughts about what the processing of prospective buyers would look like. I'll hang on to the notion that what takes place between buyer and seller is a conversation. Depending on the length of the buying cycle, it could often be described as a series of conversations.

When we are engaging someone who we suspect could use our products, services, or ideas, we are indeed in a conversation. I have no intention to rank best sales practices in order of importance, but I will share a well-founded opinion. I believe that the most important habit we can adopt in our sales career is to make every conversation meaningful. The best interactions between people take place when we start paying attention to one another. It will breathe life into relationships.

I've seen books on how to be a good conversationalist. Advice columns tell us how to say things "properly." A few years ago, "political correctness" invaded our culture and it added a self-censorship step to the already difficult task of conveying what we really want to convey. All that aside, I still rank Dale Carnegie's advice as being among the best. He said, "Show a sincere interest in the other person." I believe sincerity involves caring about the other person and what she has to say. We want to understand her. We want to do more than just listen. We want to hear.

Understanding is what lies beneath empathy, and empathy is a trait that the best in our profession don't leave home without.

I agree with self-help author Anthony Robbins who said that the quality of our lives depends on the quality of our communication. Obviously we communicate in many ways other than how we talk. Body language communicates. Actions communicate. And nothing communicates with more impact than the attitude we project, good, bad, or indifferent. In conversations between buyer and seller, it is very difficult to hide an attitude. Human beings seem to carry built in antennas.

As Natural as the Air We Breath

Anyone who sells for a living knows from daily experience that the core challenge is buyer resistance. I'm not sure everybody realizes or wants to admit that it's as natural as the air we breathe. In our conversations, we can use creativity to distinguish ourselves from "just another salesperson." We can create a favorable experience and environment. Importantly, we can provide a reassuring presence. In doing so, we have an opportunity to transcend or defuse resistance. The creative questions we ask can spark creative listening for both ourselves and our prospective buyers..

Arriving at a Better Place

When we converse, we always want the prospect to arrive at a better place. When we present a product, service, or idea, we want our prospect to reevaluate the conditions, issues, and circumstances that paint the status quo. We want her to rethink her position so that she becomes more receptive to our influence, an influence which has her best interests at heart. If we have to bring magic into the equation as if magic really does exist, I can assure you that it manifests in conveying our best intentions.

Making the Obvious Compelling

"If the prospect understood the proposition, he would not have to be sold; he would come to buy."

You may have read that quote before. I've used it twice in this book for emphasis. None of us are so old that we could have actually heard it. The speaker was John Patterson, founder of National Cash Register and an important contributor to sales education. In those good old days there were more founders than gurus!

If you engage a buyer without a proposition, all the other selling processes are merely empty. People look for value and if they can't find it in your proposition, chances are they won't buy.

"Value" is one of those nouns tossed around with abandon in advertising, sales, and marketing. In those contexts, it really refers to a perception that they can get more out of something than the dollars they part with. You hear the term "perceived value." It's important to remember that all values are perceived-not just some.

A proposition is something that is designed to morph into perceived value. Right person, right time, right place all play into it. "My Kingdom for a horse!" shouted Shakespeare's Richard the Third. In his shoes, with the horse representing escape from his demise, I would have done the same thing.

Can you imagine anybody saying that their offering is not a good value?

There are a lot of contexts in which the word, "proposition," can be used. Before your mind wanders on that, let's discuss three usages of the word as they apply to sales.

The Unique Selling Proposition

Many in sales and marketing have heard the term Unique Selling Proposition, often called USP. It refers to an identifiable difference in your product or service. In theory, we are supposed to have something that makes us pleasingly different; something the guy down the street can't provide. I want to interject that there is always something the guy down the street can't provide. He can't provide you and he can't provide me either. We should never lose sight of the idea that the person we see in the mirror just might be the identifiable difference that bags the deal.

The Emotional Selling Proposition

By volition, some salespeople take things a step further. They use an Emotional Selling Proposition, or ESP (nothing to do with the "woo woo" kind). The idea is to tweak strong emotion in the other person. Life insurance salespeople have been playing the love of family card for a very long time. Fear of loss is a prime motivator to purchase many forms of coverage. Almost any emotion can influence a decision to buy. Love, fear, envy--even anger towards a neighbor might compel someone to go out and buy some fencing.

The Obvious Selling Proposition

There is another proposition. This one tips the scales and rings the cash register. It's the Obvious Selling Proposition. The OSP represents the culmination of all those consents in the progression. It works hand in hand with the other two propositions we discussed. The reasons for buying are glaring. We have hit the sweet spot. The resistance has dissipated because there is meat in the negotiation, reasons to act now, minds to be put at ease, and perhaps an opportunity too good to pass up.

The OSP refers to a stage reached in the sales process where the "obvious" demands action. Making the decision to buy after all the facts, features, benefits, and justifications are on the table is now the "right" thing to do.

We can look beyond seeing the "unique" as merely novel and the "emotional" as merely fleeting. The "obvious" should be compelling, and that is the force behind the creative aspect of closing sales.

Saying What You Believe

All three of the propositions are directly aligned with and assigned to ourselves because we are the messengers. We are in the business of marketing ourselves just as much as marketing our products, services, and ideas. The secret for presenting ourselves in the best possible light ultimately lies in honest self expression. That means telling them what we are and what we do. But most of all, we need to tell them what we believe. We have all heard the talk about courage in sales because we face rejection. We all would want to pride ourselves on the topic of integrity. There is no better place to put both courage and integrity than in our conversations. It pays huge dividends in sales and in life to make our words impeccable.

EIGHT
Somewhere Between Hello and Yes

THE CORE CHALLENGE in the practice of selling is Resistance.

If that wasn't true, we would have the easiest job on earth. Unfortunately, they would not pay us very much. Worse--we could lose our jobs and be replaced by those take-a-number thing-a-ma-jigs that we see in supermarkets. It makes me frown that the topic of buyer resistance in sales training is mostly relegated to "handling objections" as if all we have to do is apply some fly swatter technique to a prospect's issues and concerns, and then get on to the important stuff. Common sense dictates otherwise.

A Holistic Experience

We can't shove buyer resistance under the rug. It comes with the territory. When a salesperson reaches that point in her journey where she realizes that selling is more a holistic experience than paint-by-number activity, she will be on the path that our practice of selling promises. She will know that the attainment of a desired outcome is found in the alignment of the factors and factions she faces. The steps of selling, so often referred to as the approach, the qualifying, the questioning, the presenting, the handling of objections, etc., are contained in one another. They overlap. They are inseparable. Ignore one and we ignore the whole bunch. To merely skip a step can lose a sale that would otherwise be made.

Momentum

It would be terrific if all our offers could immediately be so compelling that people can't resist us. But, in sales we are regularly challenged. Meeting those challenges is the nature of our work. We have defined the closing of a sale as a progression of consent. It also involves the maintaining of momentum.

Momentum is a force. In sales, we use creativity to bring that force into the sales conversation in such a way as to transcend, or defuse, resistance. As we discussed previously, we can distinguish ourselves from "just another salesperson" by creating a favorable experience, asking honest insightful questions that result from creative listening, and preparing ourselves with effective ways to maintain momentum. But it's not creativity alone which counters resistance. The supreme force that drives the force of momentum in sales is intention.

The Antidote for Resistance

Intention is the antidote for resistance. I would frown if that statement got swallowed up in a pool of semantics. Rather than thinking of intention merely in terms of a desired outcome, we can think of it as a driving force that dictates an outcome. Our job is to convey that intention.

What then is the intention that we need to embrace and convey to a prospective client that can be a force against natural resistance? Certainly, our experiences show us that people have a natural tendency to resist pressure. Even persistence can create resistance rather than break it down. Relentless battling for success against reluctance doesn't work very well. It's a safe assumption that our prospects are as capable as we are in protecting their own self-interest.

What we want is for the prospect to arrive at a better place. We want her to reevaluate the conditions, issues, and circumstances that cause her reluctance. We want her to rethink her position so that she becomes more receptive to our influence, an influence which has her best interests at heart.

A Smarter Conversation

Sales creativity requires tailoring the sales conversation so that it is no longer about making a sale (or resisting one). Instead, we focus on our prospect as an individual. We control the conversation only when we seek to improve the conversation. Choosing to have a "smarter conversation" is not a tactic; it's a moral decision. We build and maintain momentum focused on her wants and needs. When obvious benefits of our recommendations become compelling, the issues and concerns that feed the resistance become weakened by comparison.

A Word We Seem to be Stuck With

I'm not fond of the word "objection" as it is used in sales education, but we seem to be stuck with it. Frankly, it has been splattered around since the first sales guru put crayon to paper. It is usually joined at the hip with the word "overcome" and there are thousands of suggestions in books, courses, seminars, and, on the Internet which attempt to address "How to Overcome Objections." Frequently such guidance commences with the guide offering his chosen definition of what an objection really is. It always reminded me of how we're supposed to keep telling ourselves, while watching a scary film, "It's only a movie...it's only a movie."

Rather than pigeonholing objections into some catch-all category, I prefer to think of issues, conditions, and, circumstances when I discuss the topic of buyer resistance. If we must use the word, we need to understand objections for what they are. It will help if we empty our minds of some of the common misconceptions about them. Contrary to the popular counsel, objections are not a "request for more information." Yes, it's true that sometimes they can be treated as such. They are not "a request for assistance" as some would have us believe. Those notions will get us nowhere. Objections can only become opportunities if they are viewed in the correct light. I want to shine that light.

It might help to start with what a dictionary has to say about the meaning of the word:

Objection

n

1. an expression, statement, or feeling of opposition or dislike

2. a cause for such an expression, statement, or feeling

3. the act of objecting

Collins English Dictionary – Complete and Unabridged © HarperCollins Publishers 1991, 1994, 1998, 2000, 2003

Here, the only thing we have to focus on is the definition in the middle, which references objection as "a cause."

I don't ever want to completely devalue semantics. I am attached to the importance of context in all discussions. The context in which we want to examine objections is one where we address the topic as Stances of Resistance. They do come in all shapes and sizes.

Bear with me-- I want to share what an old pro "knight of the road" told me when I was starting out. He said, "You know, it seems for every salesperson out there, there's someone called a sales manager whose only function is to utter 'How'd you do?' when you get back into the office from a call."

Although his comment was unfair, I have to admit I smiled every time I ever heard "How'd you do?" Maybe a few of those managers never progressed very far above that skill level. Two things are certain. First, I have never been able to trace any value to "How'd you do?" Second, if the boss was asking a question, good, bad, or indifferent, one is obliged to furnish an answer (or excuse for not getting the sales). Not surprisingly, the majority of answers are appraisals of the prospective buyer's adamant resistance. Not all appraisals are kind. Perception is everything, but it's also convenient and occasionally very selective.

We only "know", or think we know, what we perceive. The perceptions of buyer resistance usually fall into one or more of the following categories as are shown below. Before we judge their accuracy, let's put them in slots. That can help us examine their validity. Our natural impulse is to search for the dissimilarity between these categories. However, let's look at the sameness, or commonalties.

Perceptions of Buyer Resistance

- **Dismissal**

    The person does not want or need what we are offering, does not want or need to do business with us, and, has no desire to reconsider.

- **Indifference**

    The person shows no interest or inclination about our product, service, presentation, conversation, or his circumstances which could be affected by what we offer.

- **Reluctance**

    The person participates in the conversation while exhibiting an attitude of reluctance. Her participation seems in conflict with our own.

- **Concerns**

    The person has specific concerns about moving forward with our offer, sometimes expressed, sometimes not.

Regardless of the disparity between the categories shown, each represents a perception of a condition or implied circumstances in which the prospective buyer will not move forward at the particular moment. It's understood, of course, that the first category (Dismissal) doesn't seem like it would contain "prospective buyers", but for now we'll delay disqualification. After all, stances can be altered or we would all be out of work. I'm sure there have been at least one or two salespeople who have reported "She threw me out!" in lieu of the more academic depiction above.

How do we know where to put our nay sayers? Where do our perceptions come from? Would it help to have more information to form a perspective? Absolutely. When we embrace and apply the understanding that honest, insightful, questions are the building blocks of a sale, our common sense will tell us. As the saying goes, "If you don't know, ask." We can begin the conversation by engaging and paying attention. We can ask questions. We can listen to the answers actively, not reactively. Our prospect will receive undivided verbal and nonverbal attention. Reactive listening, whether covert or verbalized, will often make a situation contentious. Active creative listening is about hearing what the other person is saying rather than thinking about what we're going to say next as a response (or reaction). Isn't it bothersome that so many people do the latter?

The category of Concerns resembles the popular designation, "objections." Here we want to discern what I believe is a misconception in some traditional sales training. It's widely taught that an objection and a "condition" are not to be confused with one another. Semantics again! With that lens, a condition is seen as a circumstance that we are less likely to change or remove. On the other hand, an objection is something we are supposed to "handle", "overcome", or remove. (The worst of the worst advice on the subject says that we should ignore them.) Unfortunately, those vague actions we are told to take are confusing in themselves. The truth is that an objection *is* a condition and it certainly can obstruct the completion of a sale, at least until such time as it is transcended.

Circumstances are circumstances whether we want them to be or not.

The search for an answer on how to "overcome objections" has gone on for years. Why do they keep asking, and, why do the experts keep offering their magic if the secret is out? What have we missed? Perhaps it's time to consider this:

Any attempt to overcome a prospect's objection is anti-strategic.

What do we really want to accomplish in the interest of both parties? Is our goal to overcome or remove an objection, or to dispense with one? Are we out to win a debate? Not if we're smart. We sell when we transcend objections, not when we beat them down. In reality, objections often remain, right through the act of purchasing. But--they become less of concern, because they have been weakened by comparison to the reasons and advantages for doing business (now).

Weakened by Comparison

Killing an objection can easily kill a sale. We can apply the "baby with the bathwater" metaphor or refer to the old sage of strategy, Sun Tzu, when he wrote on bamboo strips, "Keep the defeated army whole."

The message here is that other factors can tip the scales so that a prospect's concerns are deflated. Weakened by comparison!

"Your price is more than I wanted to pay." is an objection; a stance of resistance.

"Your price is more than I wanted to pay. Can you put this together to fit my budget?" is a request for assistance that comes as a result of conditions of mutual trust and respect; conditions that soften resistance.

"Your price is more than I wanted to pay, but I need to get this done, and I'm inclined to have you do the work because of your reputation for service." is an example of a weakened objection transcended by other very favorable factors.

Resistance exists in all areas of life, and nature itself, as one force among other forces. In business, all products, ideas, and services are subject to concerns. Once they take the stage, almost all are subject to the same common objections repeatedly. Rarely do they make up a long list. Many salespeople would find that they face the same six to ten objections throughout the course of their work week. Does it not make sense then for consummate sales professionals to know those concerns and be prepared to cover those issues before they arise? Preparedness *is* the most important skill in selling.

It's important for me to make something very clear. It would be blatantly presumptuous of me if I was to provide you with words to respond to your prospects' common concerns. Sales education does not come on flash cards for us to memorize. A top producer for a manufacturer of fine cutlery would not be drawing from the same pool of words as someone addressing both the needs and resistance akin to selling freight services. Key phrases and clever wording can be useful in any conversation, but they can also be manipulative and transparent. The use of generic rebuttals is for amateurs. We know that the word, "manipulation" has such a broad meaning that we can't say it's inherently bad. However, in the practice of selling, manipulative tactics are usually used to repair mistakes and omissions which already occurred. Educating oneself on the nature of your prospects' common concerns is as important as educating oneself with product knowledge. We want to be thoroughly prepared to cover those issues, ideally before they arise

The "Think it Over" Objection

No discussion on the topic of buyer resistance could be worth its salt without including the topic of the "Think it Over Objection." It seems no obstacle presents more of a challenge to so many in sales. But, the truth is it's rarely an authentic objection. It's usually a deception. So let's examine it.

When a prospect says, "I want to think it over," or something similar such as "Let me sleep on it," it usually sends one of three signals.

1. It's a convenient way to stall and not reveal the real objection or concern which often involves the costs or the perceived budget.
2. It's indicative of a hardwired factor in a person's buying habit that requires hesitation before making a final decision. Many couples or partners actually have a pact to do this when considering purchases, even when they are faced with an obvious need to make the purchase.
3. It shows a of lack full confidence, a fear of making a bad decision rather than a goal to make a good decision. Many so-called "shoppers", a label often used by retail salespeople who fail to motivate a buyer, shop out of such a fear.

Regardless of whether the prospect is actually "thinking it over", the resistance is real. Each category invites scrutiny, however.

To begin, we'll look at "the stall" described in the first case. Have you ever heard that people have two reasons for doing, or not doing, something? It's said that there is a real reason and one that sounds good. To get anywhere, we need to address the real reason. Even more important is for the prospect to admit the real reason.

Once again, it's time to re-visit and probe deeper into one of The Four Applied Understanding for success in selling. We have learned that honest insightful questions are the building blocks of sales.

An honest question is one that is asked because we want to know the answer. It is not the rhetorical kind which is really just a statement in disguise. It is not a question that we already know, or think we know the answer to. It is not a leading question, best suited for attorneys. An intrinsic or insightful question is one that is asked so that we can dig to the heart of the matter. As professionals worthy of trust, we don't deny ourselves the right to ask honest insightful questions in search of honest answers. We must ask them.

Why do I dwell on the above? Our studies have revealed that there is a common and transparent "technique", designed to ferret out real objections, which is still taught in countless training courses and books on selling. It consists of a series of leading questions that are supposed to lead to an admission by the prospect that the real concern is about money. Although cost often is a factor, such tactics are not consistent with the honest and intrinsic nature of the type of questions we should be asking.

If we believe that the issues are about budget or money, or anything else, we should ask about what we want to know, direct and to the point. There is no reason to suspend the instincts that tell us to ask the right questions.

In the second category we have prospects that cling to a personal policy of hesitating before they make a final decision to buy. In my own experiences, I have detected a strong personal belief in that buying habit among those who practice it. Years ago, I made a decision to honor those beliefs when I encountered them. Looking back, I can say that I have no regrets for that decision. I focus on creating the best possible experience I can for a prospective client. I do not focus on challenging the core beliefs of the person I choose to sell to.

The third factor, a prospect's of lack of confidence and fear of making a bad decision, has become as prevalent as ever in today's world. The variety of solutions, products, and, services, can be confusing and staggering with daily advances in technology and distribution. It's a sign of the times. Conditions of mutual trust and respect have a huge role in transcending a buyer's lack of confidence. Just as important is the overall experience a salesperson provides.

Perhaps there is no better question to ask a prospect than, "What would you like to accomplish?"

In Chapter Thirteen, we'll talk more about the "Think it Over" scenario. In this chapter, I began with the statement that the core challenge in selling is resistance. We inspected some perceived categories; perceived in the eye of the seller. It was noted that, by its nature, the elements of selling, for a master practitioner, are holistic--always connected.

Qualifying a Prospect

The topic of qualifying a prospect belongs in any discussion about buyer resistance. For too long, it has been improperly set apart as if it involves a separate step. Nowhere is the interconnectedness of the holistic experience of a sales conversation more evident. Qualifying plays into just about everything we want to accomplish in front of a prospect. Once again, the factors between buyer and seller are never isolated.

It helps to get things rolling with a definition, so let's throw the first question on the table. What exactly is "qualifying?" Here we can turn to what most primers on selling have taught for years. They explain that qualifying consists of determining whether a prospect is ready, willing, and, able to buy.

Ready, willing, and, able? That's an acceptable model. We can, however, probe that explanation deeper, and then the choice becomes whether to dwell on it or not. I suggest that there is more to the picture.

Think on these things. If it has been determined (not assumed) that a prospect is ready, willing, and able to buy, are we ready to sell? Are we willing to sell? Are we able to sell? Are we ready to offer the best possible solution for the client? Do we want him as a client? Are we able to sell what he wants? (Do we have the goods?) Could we hurt our position with an existing client if we brought this client aboard? Is there a conflict of interest? Would this new client need such high maintenance that the profit would diminish or even produce a loss? If the buyer prospect promises something in return for a price concession, is he ready, willing, and, able to keep the promise?

Have I muddied the water with such questions? It's not my intention. I have one reason for that mishmash and it is not to rain on anyone's parade. I accept ready, willing, and able as a fundamental working model for qualifying. It represents a standard. However, we need to take into account that personal standards differ from person to person, and, company standards differ from company to company.

In my own library, I have an excellent, somewhat autobiographical, book on selling by David Cowper, titled *Mega-Selling: Secrets of a Master Salesman (Published by John Wiley and Sons)*. In the text, Cowper, a hugely successful insurance professional, shares his own standard for qualifying. Whether or not his standard becomes a standard for you or me to follow, it does serve to deepen our understanding of the continuous qualifying responsibility in selling. His words shed new light for me. For years, I have suggested to aspiring salespeople that they memorize them. Here are Cowper's five questions to ask oneself when evaluating a prospect:

1. Will I do business with them?

2. Will they do business with me?

3. Do I realize their need?

4. Do they realize their need?

5. Can they pay the freight?

How do we choose our requirements for qualifying? Whatever our decision, it's important that it is based on equally an important decision. We will decide to spend our precious time with the activities and people and prospects that will give us the best results.

The Most Powerful Word

With all that said, it's time to come back to the category of resistance that we referred to as Dismissal. I can't think of a better thought to start with than this. The most powerful word in any language just might be "No!" (Exclamation point is mine with the hope it gets the right effect.)

Okay, I'll admit that "no" may not be the most powerful word that we use or hear, but it certainly can change relationships. It can pull people apart. It can bring people closer. Most importantly, for the sake of these discussions on selling, it can point us in the right direction.

"Maybe" rarely points us anywhere except out the door. "No" sets us back on course; it is valuable information.

In the Dismissal category, the following description was used: The person does not want or need what we are offering, does not want or need to do business with us, and has no desire to reconsider. The accepted standard of qualification, ready, willing, and able, immediately disqualifies that individual on the basis of unwillingness and non-readiness, and, we don't even know if he is able. My personal standard for qualification would not see me waste time trying to sell this person. Can he be sold? Possibly the answer is yes. Should I attempt to transcend the resistance or do I move on? If I focus my energies on converting that non-buyer, or not-buyer (take your pick), I'm spending time in an area with the least possible return over the long run.

Qualifying really looks an awful lot like disqualifying, doesn't it? I have yet to have an argument with anyone who casually described selling or sales prospecting as "sorting."

The great sales authority of years gone by, Fred Herman, put it so wonderfully when he quoted scriptures, "Why seek ye the living among the dead?"

Indifference

It's time to get among the living. We have much resistance to transcend. Can we enter the world of the indifferent prospect and find ways to meet that formidable challenge? Or--does that world really exist? For years, the topic of the indifferent prospect has been the most difficult area to explore in sales education. The experts will give us blank stares, or perhaps excuse themselves because they're running late to teach a seminar.

Could it possibly be that the display of an attitude of indifference is really a stylized form of reluctance? When we showed categories of resistance, we referred to them as perceptions; no mention of reality.

Once again we want to stay in context and the following dictionary definition works quite well: *Indifference: Marked by impartiality; unbiased.*

It doesn't look scary to me. On the other hand, if my mental image of indifference was one of smugness on the part of the prospect, it has dissolved. I see no "dismissal" rearing its head. As a matter of fact, maybe I like what I see. We are, after all, change masters, aren't we?

What if we viewed all prospects at the time we first encounter them as unbiased; neutral? Would that make the task ahead of us harder or easier? Here's a better (honest and insightful) question: Would that perspective bring us more into focus and ensure a greater effectiveness?

The answer to that second question is an unqualified yes. I wonder if we have just put a damper on assumptive selling. I may get letters on that one.

Who's Hot?

If you are one of the people who have scratched their heads on the topic of resistance like I did for a long time, then I invite you to think on some things. The next conversation we have with a prospective buyer will occur for one of two reasons. Either we found her or she found us. We might already have the notion that the person who comes to us is a hotter prospect than the one that we had to go out and find. And, of course, "hotter" would appear to calibrate very low on the indifference scale if we still believed that such a scale exists. However, what we believe about such matters is a huge factor in how well we're going to do in our sales career. We hear a lot of talk about the importance of attitude in selling. Too often it's described as if it were a tool; something we can keep in our briefcase to take along on a sales call. It's so easy to think that we need to adjust our attitude to fit the prospect at hand. But, attitude is not so much a tool as it is the sum of our personal beliefs. Therefore it's not something we can alter, should we be apprised of the need to alter, unless we are willing to examine our beliefs and dissect them. Trust me; the process will bear more fruit then the common practice of faking it. Another one of those wise persons once said that the first step towards wisdom is calling things by their right name. Does it seem possible now that, with all those questions and very few answers about indifference in selling, the sales training experts were chasing a red herring? Hasn't it been about Reluctance all along? And-- isn't reluctance usually about resistance to change; about the traps of inertia where prospects want to keep doing what they have been doing all along, even if it's nothing.

Inertia is a word many of us learned in high school physics class. It refers to the resistance of a body to changes in its momentum. In our practice, it translates well into a prevalent factor of complacency. "But that's what we've always bought," says the prospective client who perceives no distinction or value between what we are selling and their existing product or service.

Reluctance is not based in logic. It lies entrenched in our prospect's perception. In approaching reluctance, the sales professional cannot be expected to understand the psychological considerations that are tied to changing an attitude. We are not psychologists. What we can do is gain permission to ask honest questions that will increase our understanding of the prospect's specific needs and wants. We can observe the status quo, and the problems that can exist or grow because of the status quo. What's working? What's not working? Is the prospect open to change the latter? What would motivate that willingness to change? Those questions are paramount to a strategy that lies at the heart of consultative selling.

Honest insightful questions can raise the level of awareness of a prospect's satisfaction and dissatisfaction with his current circumstances. They can reveal the cost of leaving things unchanged, and, promote the desire to facilitate change. This is momentum that can accelerate. We want to align with the prospective buyer's desires with the products, service, and ideas that make up our portfolio.

I've given no secret sauce recipes, no fancy tactics, no clever words, and no ingenious rebuttals to use in the perceived battle for our prospective buyer's mind. Instead, I've shared understandings that took years to manifest in my own mind. We hear about the fear of rejection among salespeople, a subject that's beaten to death. We are asked to summon our courage and not take things personally. Good advice, always. But there are better ways to show our courage and the best way is to get in touch with the artists within ourselves, express what we need to express, and let the cards fall where they may.

Go Ahead! Try this Experiment.

I have another story to tell. I once wrote to a man I admire as a leader in sales education, asking for his participation on a project I was working on. I closed with "Best regards," two spaces above my signature. He wrote back, regretting that he was unable to help. He made a point to thank me for my "regards."
Ouch!

He closed with "I appreciate you," two spaces above his signature. That's a closing that I have used in all my correspondence since.

I look back on the words I've written here, and what I said about intention being the true antidote for buyer resistance. I reread those words I wrote about dismissal, which might be the toughest form of rejection we have to face in our work. It prompts me to offer the reader a proposition. I propose the following experiment for bringing out that sales artist within you. The next time you face that dismissal, and as you are about to walk away, turn around and say to that human being, "I want you to know that I came here with the very best of intentions."

Live and work to make that statement true.

I appreciate you.

NINE
Making a Proposal a Proposition

"IF THE PROSPECT understood the proposition, he would not have to be sold; he would come to buy."

That's a famous quote from John Patterson, the founder of National Cash Register, and the "father of American salesmanship." I'm tempted to give him some latitude for exaggeration, but the more I think about it, he may not need it. Let's you and I take him seriously on that.

Buyers don't buy a proposal, written or otherwise. They buy the proposition. That's why any proposal worth the paper it's written on must contain a proposition. As we discussed in the last chapter, it's the proposition that counts. Without it, we're not selling anything, because we have nothing to sell.

Before I go further on this topic, I find it necessary to say some things upfront.

First, I realize that not everybody in sales is required to provide written proposals to prospective buyers. I also

MAKING A PROPOSAL A PROPOSITION

know that some people provide them out of choice in circumstances where the buyer does not require one.

Next, I'm fully aware that not everyone in sales has excellent copy writing skills.

Finally, some requests for quotations are issued by organizations that have strict formats for constructing such quotes. In some cases, the seller is given a form by the buyer to complete with only the details described in front of the empty spaces.

All of that is true and sometimes we are bound by limitations; our own, and, those imposed by others.

In spite of all of the above, we cannot let our own creativity in sales be hobbled. If we do, we risk our potential. With that said, I want to discuss propositions and how they relate to proposals.

Our Process Meets Their Process

In business to business selling, many buyers are regimented into a fixed buying format specifically for their own convenience. That does not necessarily mean that it is a good process. Cutting to the chase or getting to the bottom line for expediency is a prime cause of missed opportunities for making better purchases. When salespeople religiously align with such bureaucratic rituals among buyers, they sacrifice their own creative devises and put themselves at the mercy of unfriendly inertia.

A Sales Letter in Disguise

A well-written proposal is a sales letter in disguise. The driving force in any proposition can be summed up in two words: "compelling offer." Unfortunately, we hear that words, "adding value," used so often among marketing types it's easy to ignore the meaning. I prefer to refer to adding value as "sweetening the pot."

The sales industry is not crowded with good copy writers. That's a good thing for you and I. Few people know that proposal writing is copy writing and the best proposals reflect the skills of good copy writing because that is conversation also.

I'm not blind to the fact that I've introduced a new challenge. I encourage salespeople to become skilled at good copy writing. The pay-off is immense.

Emphasizing Features and Benefits

The best of the best in selling will disassociate themselves from the norm. Submitting a written quotation that merely outlines price, goods, service, warranty, and/or scope of work might well align with what the prospective buyer expects. However, the overriding best practice in sales is to always strive to exceed expectations. A proposal, if constructed creatively, can distinguish a company or representative by offering a benefit not readily available elsewhere. Never should any written communication be perceived as if it were a rubber stamped form. Instead, a well-written proposal can emphasize features and benefits like quality of service and support, prompt delivery, and time sensitive offers that harbor no extra costs.

Headlines in Our Proposal

Every request for quotation is an opportunity for us to tell our story, not to align with a buyer's mundane or dogmatic process. What do all well-constructed sales letters have in common? They use headlines. Why? Headlines are magnets. All the best sales copy writers agree; people read headlines with a sharper eye than they read the copy that follows.

Staying Creative and Ahead of the Competition

It's important to know that the actual process of designing the customer value proposition is an ongoing process. Our competition is likely to offer the same type of enhancements over time. In fact, they'll be looking to offer more attractive offers. This means that a company's brain trust must constantly be searching for ways to improve the value of customer benefits so they can maintain their advantage. A well-crafted value proposition makes it possible to not rely solely on price to win the business. Little extras count and they should be highlighted in our proposal.

We Decide Where the Selling Conversation Ends.

It is a "best practice" in sales to make every conversation meaningful. Sometimes we have to interrupt the buying process in order to get it where we want it to go. We decide where the conversation ends. So long as we are fair and ethical, we can shape our own protocol. Requests for quotations that describe the buyer's requirements and specifications are not always etched in stone. Nor are they always accurate. More often than not, negotiation takes center stage.

Without a strong and differentiating proposition all selling processes are sterile. With one, the seller can occupy the driver's seat. Then "negotiation" simply takes the form of "modification". Modify the terms, modify the offer, modify the quantity, etc.--all to reach accord and closure.

Better Than the Next Guy

As I've repeated often throughout these pages, we're always being compared. The overriding practice of always exceeding expectations will find fertile ground where ever we apply it. As I have attempted to point out, the mundane tasks of writing proposals can be opportunities to shine.

So--let's shine!

TEN
Should We "Always be Closing?"

NOW WE COME to a topic I have conflicting viewpoints about. But first a story.

When I was a young, over-my-head, unqualified, Peter-Principled sales manager, I borrowed a sales training film and featured it at our weekly sales meeting. (I don't want to be too hard on myself--my intentions were noble.) It was largely dramatized with actors showing how to "ask for the order." In fact, *Ask for the Order* was the name of the film. It was so unrealistic and fictional that today I still grimace at the thought that I asked my staff to watch that stuff. Now, when I refer to "asking for the order," that's exactly what they had these actors doing. When we say, as was portrayed in the film, "Can I have an order from you, Sir/Madam?" it indicates an imploring or beseeching manner that somehow doesn't fit as follow-up or conclusion to a skillful sales conversation.

I know that "closing" is a progression of consent--not an event. I also know that a "closing question" can take many forms. There are always better ways to ask for anything. I'm reminded of a young woman who asked me, "Can I be your contractor?" She sold me, but not because it was clever and professional although it was. Her "way" was to ask for a business relationship. One has to know the difference. The people who produced that film didn't know the difference.

Here's what I'm getting at. The advice that we should "always be closing" increases in value in direct proportion to our level of understanding of the concept. The same can be said for much of the rhetoric thrown at us from books, blogs, and well meaning sales coaches. It helps when some of the advice givers understand the material themselves. In fairness, some do understand and they were there to help me understand too.

Okay--so I'm as guilty as many are, posting a question while harboring a bias towards certain answers. I coined the term, "parrot platitudes," in what I have written. I got tired of the cliché's and memes in sales lore that popped up with regularity. In the preface of my first book I spoke with sharp tongue about what passed for sales education in some quarters.

Our topic, "always be closing," is at the mercy of context and interpretation. For example, if I was in a high school style debating contest, I could easily take either the affirmative or negative sides effectively. In the former, closing would be in the context of a progression, a series of agreements. In the latter (the negative) the context would be shown as "attempts", i.e., keep trying to close. ("There is no 'try', Luke.") It would not be hard to paint a silly picture of that scenario.

To always be closing in the right context and with the correct understanding is strategic. As we will discuss in the next chapter, strategy is about putting things in place to affect a desired outcome. A salesperson's use of tactics without strategy, on the other hand, often consists of attempting to repair what came before--or what failed to come before.

Let's examine further. Should we always be closing? The answer is yes providing we know what closing actually is. The answer is no if you're among those who have not grasped what closing looks like. In the latter case, you'll only make matters worse. How many times have you heard that there are "secrets" to closing sales? Closing secrets--that's enticing! It's only natural to want to be let in on the secrets. Wouldn't it be horrible to spend our whole lives in sales and not be privy to how to actually make money at it?

Some of us became familiar with the phrases, "closing tactics" and "closing techniques." Is a "closing question" the *coup d'état* to a masterful sales presentation? Or, is it supposed to be the salvager of a weak one?

Salespeople sometimes get chastised by their "superiors" for not "asking for the order." Is asking for the order the close? Some of us have been taught a linear sales process that ends with "the close." (AIDCA, anyone?) That would make it an event, wouldn't it?

I'm just loaded with questions, aren't I? The truth is that closing of a sale is not an event. It is a progression. One of the Four Applied Understandings that you are now studying states: Closing is a progression of consent.

Now--for those who are still hung up on the old perspectives, it's time to pull this idea apart and have an even closer look. Remember the AIDCA model we discussed earlier? Well, I'm bold enough to say it's flawed. Remember how the first "A" in the acronym stands for Attention, something we want to gain? It should stand for

SHOULD WE "ALWAYS BE CLOSING?"

Agreement. That's because the best way to get positive attention is to establish common ground early. Establishing common ground early is the first step in a progression of consent. That's what closing is: a series of agreements that lead to a desired outcome. Can we now say that we should always be progressing in that series of agreements? To once again use a favorite catch phrase of mine, I believe the obvious has become compelling.

Does that give credibility, finally, to that platitude, Always Be Closing? I think it does. With that said, my feet are getting tired on this soapbox.

ELEVEN
Putting Things in Place

CLOSING A SALE is not a tactical maneuver. It is a strategic experience.

Strategy is one of the most misunderstood words in our language. As a result, the words, "strategic" and "tactical" are often wrongly interchanged. They will not be mingled in that manner throughout these pages. A mentor of mine, a renowned expert on the subject, told me on a few occasions that one of the best parts of strategy is that most people don't understand it which gives those that do understand it a huge advantage.

This is not the place to completely cover the tenets of strategy. A fellow by the name of Sun Tzu did that over 2500 years ago on bamboo strips. But, I will offer the following working definition to suffice for these discussions. Strategy consists of putting things in place to achieve a desired outcome. That is a simple and effective way to think about it.

The Four Applied Understandings that we refer to throughout these pages happen to reside in the realm of strategy. I think of them as "meta-strategy" which is a term

I coined. They exist as an overriding framework for how we can think about selling. One of those understandings is that closing is a progression of consent. I look upon a progression of consent as the process of putting agreements in place by targeting them one at a time. I know that if every required agreement was in place, there would be no reason for an "event" that others call "a close." That's because a natural and easy conclusion would exist. Some people erroneously believe that a "closing question" and a close are synonymous. So--they think the question should be tricky or clever. However, it's folly to think about closing as one singular big stroke (He shoots; he scores!) That gives rise to the misguided notion that closing is a tactic. How often have we heard the term, "closing tactics?" But if the salesperson has followed a progression of consent, the "call to action" would be there in its silence. The sale is there for the taking. The signature on the dotted line is a formality, not the result of a heroic maneuver.

Is consent all that has to be put in place in a sales conversation? Did I just hear the word, "rapport?"

I have been hearing about rapport ever since I ventured into sales education. As a matter of fact, I'm constantly told it's something we are supposed to "build." With all respect to those who pet goldfish and admire bowling trophies, I much prefer harmony over rapport. In the conversation between buyer and seller, harmony is exemplified by conditions of mutual trust and respect. I focus a lot on the word, "mutual." The harmony and conditions of mutual trust and respect allow us to enter the other person's world. They are indicative of forms of consent in its own right.

We can disengage from the notion that closing comes at the tail end. We can think of closing a sale as a holistic practice. We can see that the harmony of mutual trust and respect is something we seek to "put into place" because we see it as part of a strategy--not an isolated shot-in-the-dark tactic? It's not a sin to suspend our belief in rapport in favor of seeking, identifying, and participating in conditions of mutual trust and respect.

It will work wonders.

TWELVE
Scripts

BACK WHEN BUSINESS format radio stations were popular, I was interviewed on the topic of "salesmanship." Halfway through the session, the moderator asked me what I thought about "canned pitches."

I told him I never used the words, "canned" or "pitch." I suggested that he might be referring to prepared presentations. When his flushing subsided, I told him that I was neither for nor against prepared presentations in sales. I couldn't help but think that, with his choice of words, he was trying to influence my answer. Perhaps in his own dealings with salespeople he had encountered someone whose rehearsed conversation seemed transparent. Although I don't remember my exact comments in that interview, I do recollect my thoughts on the topic and they really haven't changed much.

You can't cover much ground in a twenty minute interview. When I suggested the term, "prepared presentations," I knew that I was guilty of contributing to a narrow view, much like that of the interviewer with his "pitch" and "canned" references. A presentation is only one part of what might take place in a sales interview. We do much more than just "present" products, services, ideas, and the features and benefits that adjoins them. Also, we can't lump all selling situations into one neat pile. There are simple transactional sales and there are complex sales. The time span from "hello" to a signed contract can vary from minutes to months. In some cases, an entire complex sales project could take years.

When we talk to people about what we do for a living, we're at the mercy of their preconceptions of what selling is about. A lot of lay people don't realize, for example, that questions and listening are vital ingredients. If we're going to address the pros and cons of modes of preparation, the topic of prepared questions belongs somewhere in the forefront of the discussion.

At least two things are certain. Selling is conversation and preparedness is a necessary skill.

Here I'll take time out for some career advice. If you start a sales job with a company that requires you to learn and use a prepared script or presentation, I highly recommend that you follow orders. It's important for me to express that and get it out of the way. We are on dangerous ground when we demonstrate an unwillingness to follow an employer's instructions. When we become superstars, they give us some leeway. When our name goes on the building, we'll continue to do what got us there.

The fact that I'm neither for nor against scripts suggests that I'm passive enough for readers to draw their own conclusions on their value. I sincerely hope they will. However, my neutrality might give a clue that my emotions are mixed. I'm not waffling here. I do know that sometimes two opposing viewpoints can both have merit. I'll give two examples, drawn from many that I have witnessed, which contribute to the mix.

I once mentored a young man who had entered the life insurance and financial planning field with a very large company. As a requirement for working at the company, he had to memorize, word for word, a seventeen minute talk which he would have to deliver to each and every prospect that he gained an appointment with. I had the opportunity to listen to the talk several times as he rehearsed. In addition, I acquired a written copy of the script. I drew some conclusions that I hold to this day.

My first and lasting impression was that his talk was solely for the purpose of projecting an image. Some people might call that posturing. The young fellow was using words and delivering information that was as meaningless to him as they were indecipherable to the listener. He didn't have a clue as to what he was talking about and I am sure that the company who made him deliver that talk knew he did not have a clue. Their philosophy was that it didn't matter; just get the words out.

As far as I'm concerned, what I listened to was double speak about the company he represented. For example, the following words were taken right from his script: *"If ranked by assets, (my company) would place sixth among the top fifteen industrials."*

What in the hell does that mean?

But hold on! This young guy memorized the talk. He delivered it again and again. That was his job. That is what his employer required. In time, he built an outstanding, financially successful, career using that approach which was called "the funnel talk." Eventually, he went on to train and mentor others. To this day he says that he could not have launched his life's work without that script. I'm inclined to believe him even though I know that one prepared talk does not a successful career make. If it did, we could dispense with all the other chapters in this book.

Did I just hear someone say it's really just a numbers game? Was the example one that depicted the practice of throwing enough stuff against enough walls?

It would be a stretch for me believe that there were many prospects that our young man approached who were able to assimilate much of was contained in his seventeen minute soliloquy. I seriously doubt that whatever messages were in the talk could be captured when you consider the average person's attention span. Please don't ask me what that span is according to statistics. I haven't a clue. I'll let my doubt override the necessity to look it up. However, facts don't lie. The fellow built an extraordinary career.

For my second example, I'll use a story from my own sales background. Early in my career, I worked for a large international publishing company. I called on prospects from pre-set appointments that originated from mail-in requests for information. It was one of my first experiences with lead generation from direct response marketing, a field I would eventually specialize in. New to the company, I attracted management's attention with my superior sales results from the leads that were provided to me. They wanted to know what this fresh face was doing to get all those sales. Then I got a phone call from a sales legend with the company who now served as a regional vice president. Part of his legacy was that he was the creator of a very successful scripted presentation that bore his name. He said that he wanted to visit my area and accompany me on calls.

Obviously I became excited about the opportunity. As one might expect, I was more than a little bit nervous.

I had heard his presentation on tape and I had become enthralled with some of the expressions and phraseology he used. I had made notes. I decided to adopt some of the material to use in my own interviews with prospective buyers. Some--not all.

When it came time for my first interview with a prospect in front of the vice president, these were the first words I spoke, drawn perfectly from my esteemed observer's script: *"(The Company) has been around forever; actually we date back to the nineteenth century. The reason we made changes was that our editors felt that we could get more information across in an easier, more concise, manner. What they decided to do was break the material into three sections."*

Those were the exact words that began the presentation that I had studied. I was saying them in front of the very man that had composed them.

Then, I got off the prescribed tract. I continued my conversation in the style that I had been using successfully. Things went fine. It was not a difficult sale. We left the prospect with a signed order in my briefcase. Certainly I had impressed my visiting vice president and I was anxious to hear his praise when he seated himself in the passenger side of my car.

He didn't waste any time. His words still stick with me better than any words from the tape I watched. He said, "Gary, I see that you must have done some study on my presentation. Well, if you're going to use it, then use it word for word." Then he said with more emphasis, "All the paraphrasing is already done."

Ouch!

Why the mixed emotions on this topic? Let's dissect. On one hand, I have no doubt that there is considerable merit in prepared conversation. However, in the examples I provided of scripted lines, they did not necessarily convey relevant information. In fact, I believe that the real intent--one that has succeeded--was to posture. Relevancy did not matter. What mattered was a conversational tone, albeit rehearsed, that projected an image of competence, reliability, and professionalism. In the case of the young insurance salesman, substance relative to the prospect's situation or circumstance was mostly absent. In the latter example--my own--I may have benefited from my swiped opening remarks because they were conversational, but they had little to do with the conversation which followed. In both cases, it was the posturing that set the stage for rapport.

Am I alone in my mixed feelings? Posturing sometimes has sort of a negative connotation, doesn't it? In many life situations, such a dim view is founded. In sales, when done with strategic intent, it certainly can be effective to project a certain image. To present oneself in a favorable light is a worthwhile personal marketing activity. It becomes a bad practice if we neglect the need to tell the truth.

Consider that the opening scripted words in both examples were not about features, benefits, or what the seller could do for the buyer. They were simply references that demonstrated the salesperson's knowledge with the intent of creating an expectation that a meaningful conversation would follow. I'm not willing to condemn that. However, even when we posture and disregard relevancy, I would condemn a departure from the truth.

SCRIPTS

Let's sum up, regardless of whether our emotions remain mixed. If we can sort through the mixed bag of perspectives on the topic of prepared presentations and scripted conversations, we can end up dead center on one of the Four Applied Understandings for success in sales. Preparedness is indeed the most important skill in selling. I see no moral difference between a planned encounter and a script just because the latter is more rigidly adhered to. The use of either must be judged by their effectiveness. I've used the word "posturing" because I've witnessed so many prepared conversations devoted to projecting an image of competence, reliability, and professionalism. (Interestingly, to take a stand against posturing would be posturing in its own right.) We know that we must sell ourselves while selling our products, services, or ideas. Preparing to achieve that with a careful plan seems extremely logical.

THIRTEEN
Do They Really Think it Over?

I'M OUT FOR bear on this topic!

I learned long ago that "no" is a very powerful word. Some people think it's the most powerful word in any language. Maybe that's why prospects avoid using the word. Instead a lot of them use "I want to think it over" in place of "no". The cash register remains still and silent in either case. I did an Internet search to see how many sites would come up for "how to handle the think it over objection." After scrolling links for ten minutes I stopped counting. All that my effort provided was evidence that there are lots of people that actually believe that those words are a real objection. Let me qualify what I've said. There certainly are real objections. "I don't like the color," or, "These shoes are too tight," are real objections. So is, "I don't want to do business with you because I don't trust you."

At face value, "I want to think it over," is a statement that implies the prospect has listened to your offer and now wants to take the time to deliberate before she commits. If that's an objection then we have to count "no" as an

DO THEY REALLY THINK IT OVER?

objection and, the last time I looked, it was in the rejection column.

I don't have the statistics--nobody does--but I reckon that authentic deliberation follows in less than one percent of those cases.

Here's a familiar scenario:

Salesperson: "Hello, Fred, it's Tom from Acme calling just to follow up on our meeting last Tuesday. I know you said you wanted to think my offer over. Are you ready to move ahead?"

Prospect: "Oh, hello, Tom. Gee--you know what? I've been so busy--things are crazy here--that I really haven't had time to give it much thought. But, listen, I'll let you know either way when I decide. Thanks for calling."

Let's kick it up a notch and see what Einstein had to say about chasing red herrings. He said you can't solve a problem at the level of the problem. Okay--back to earth among us mortals. When a prospect wants to think your offer over, the solution is not to attempt to overcome that stance of resistance. The prospect might just get the notion that the salesperson doesn't want him to think it over and then ask himself, "Hmm...Why is that?"

The plain ugly fact is that the prospect isn't buying. So-- where does the problem lie? It lies in the fact that the salesperson has not given the prospect adequate reasons to buy. Maybe the reasons do not exist for some people we think are prospects.

At this point, let's trash all of the tactics we've heard about handling "think it over." Tactics in sales are almost always used to repair what came before. Instead, an honest insightful question is called for. In sales, we have the option to use two words that are very powerful in their own right. They are, "What's missing?"

Ask that question: "What's missing?" Let's ask it every time we are told by a prospect that he wants to "think it over."

It's been said many times that people have two reasons for doing, or not doing, anything--the real reason, and the one that sounds good.

Never doubt for a minute that something is missing because if something wasn't missing we would have the sale, and the "think it over" impediment would not have stirred discussions to the degree that it has.

You and I aren't above formulating a catchy and clever rule. Let's make one up! How's this?

When we hit a roadblock with a prospect, we ask an honest question.

That has a nice ring to it!

FOURTEEN
Following Through

SECOND EFFORT IS a 1968 sales training film starring Vince Lombardi, the Hall of Fame head coach of the Green Bay Packers. It has been called a "classic" and still regarded by some experts as the best sales training film of all time. Almost a half century later, the film is still used in leadership and management courses.

Not too long ago, I had the opportunity to visit Lambeau Field in Green Bay and take a tour of the complete facilities prior to watching the Packers play a game on Sunday. The feeling and aura was overwhelming and I know that many others have described their visit as almost a spiritual experience. Lombardi was about winning, but, more importantly, he preached the necessity to take the steps and pay the price that lead to winning.

In the minds of most of the people I talk to in sales, the thoughts of "follow up" flow when they hear the words, "second effort." Specifically, the act of following up with an active prospect seems to imply an attempt to salvage a sale that thus far has failed to materialize. I have thoughts about the reasons why that perception is so common.

It's an unfortunate reality that traditional sales training is still fettered on the "one-call closes" that were the desired outcomes of direct sales organizations more than a half century ago. It is absurd how little regard is given to the length of the selling cycle in situations where a quick decision could be disastrous for all parties concerned. In a previous chapter, you met three successful salespeople from the financial planning, media advertising, and, web marketing arenas, who would be repulsed by writing a premature sale. Worse, they would be rebuked by most of their prospects for attempting to write one. There are simple sales and there are those that are complex and there are some that are in between. The "sales industry" is so diversified and multifaceted today that the term itself is hardly appropriate. Relationship, consultative, and, account management responsibilities take up a huge slice of the pie. The progression of consent that puts signed contracts into the in-basket can take place over a series of conversations that range from few to many.

Second Effort was about persistence and that's an admirable trait in selling and in life. I suspect Lombardi's words and participation made the adrenaline flow for many aspiring salespeople. I know I was affected that way.

I titled this chapter to differentiate a strategic model for "following through" from the tired advice that we should be "following up" because I promised that this was a book that focused on understanding. It's only fair that, if I'm about to preach on this critical topic, I should come right out and disclose four of my core beliefs.

- I believe that salespeople that begin a call with "I'm calling to follow up...", or, "I'm calling to touch

base..." are salespeople that don't know what they're doing.
- I believe in The Purposeful Call.
- I believe in making promises and keeping them.
- I believe that when persistence is perceived as intrusiveness, our efforts will fail.

I encourage people in sales who suffer from "fear of rejection" or "call reluctance" to make those beliefs their own because of their healing properties.

Making Promises: The Strategy of Following Through

I want to introduce a strategic model for following up with prospects and buyers. One of the points we have touched on is that strategy is a process that consists of putting pieces in place that will result in a desired outcome. The "piece" that I recommend be put in place consistently, as a first step towards following up, or, following through, is a promise.

Promise Generation

For use in courses and seminars we coined the term "promise generated." It describes a contact with prospect or client that has been generated by a promise the salesperson has made. In simple terms, it affords the salesperson an opportunity to perpetuate the engagement with a buyer in a meaningful way. To us, a promise is a tool and we should strive to find ways to make them and keep them.

There are four worthy reasons behind this strategy.

1. It makes the call a purposeful call.
2. It makes the call an expected, permission based, contact.
3. It demonstrates a promise kept (often with additional pertinent information).
4. Lastly, and most important, it continues and renews the sales process and selling effort.

Once again, it boils down to maintaining momentum, the force that drives the progression of consent called closing sales.

Now it's time for the caveat. Not all promises are welcome. Not all promises will generate a positive response, spoken or unspoken, from a prospect. "I'll call you in a few days for your decision." can not only leave a prospect cold, but also put a perceived burden on her shoulders. "I'll call you next week, just to follow up." is pure fluff. "I'll call you after you've had a chance to talk it over." is adding encouragement to natural buyer resistance which we covered earlier. "I'll call you if I can come up with anything better." shifts all leverage to the buyer, assuming the seller had any to begin with.

A promise to a prospective buyer should always be built around furnishing further information to the buyer that is not on hand at the moment. That is the rule that makes this strategic model work. The promise and deliverance of further information maintains and builds momentum. It can create a frame of loyalty in the mind of the buyer. And, it can enhance the partnership between buyer and seller.

Sound strategy will always take precedent over cheap tactics or an isolated technique.

FIFTEEN
Yes, We Need to Know

MCDONALD'S SELLS MORE cheeseburgers than anyone else in the world.

Next time you visit one, if you're so inclined, try asking two questions of the person behind the counter:

How much is a cheeseburger? What's on a cheeseburger?

You may get a blank stare like I did, because the person doesn't know. Neither could she find the price on the big menu above her. (That in itself is a challenge because the price appeared to be cleverly hidden juxtaposed next to the cheeseburger "meal" at several times the price.)

"Need to know" is a business philosophy which is practiced in a lot of management circles. The employee "needs to know" how to push those buttons on her screen. Product knowledge is expendable. But the young person who waited on me is denied the value of incremental learning which includes what's going on around her. She will make a much better doctor, teacher, public official, nurse, accountant, law enforcement officer, etc., if her knowledge isn't contained by those who would turn her into a robot.

That's not REALLY a little thing. It's about the future. Her future and ours.

SIXTEEN
An Axe to Grind

NOWADAYS THE BEST practitioners in sales are artists. The same could be said for many fields of endeavor. It is the artists that are connecting regardless of how they make their way in the world. Selling is one of those ways, and some people practice it in an artful manner. Many among the top of their profession have internalized recognizable patterns in their dealings with prospects and buyers. However, they rarely allow their ability to recognize patterns trap them into assumptions. They know that no two situations are exactly alike. It keeps them curious and curiosity feeds creativity.

Regardless of what the textbooks and piles of white papers would have us believe, there is no universal buying process. A lot of selling methodologies are constructed as if there was. That thought is not meant to darken the spirits of men and women who have invested time and energy into learning and conforming to systems of selling that are designed to achieve the highest results from the market they work in. I know from experience that many of those formats work and work very well.

The person who sits across the table from us in the role of buyer is unique. No two people that we sell will have the exact same agenda or conditions of satisfaction to meet. The head of purchasing for a large manufacturer does not have the same vested interest in the bottom line as the owners of that company. Partners in a marriage will seldom share the exact same emotional attachment to a home they are considering purchasing. The person who has incurred a loss is of a different mindset than the person who will consider preventing such a loss.

Sales experts preach that we must find the pain among our prospects, assess their needs, determine their wants, overcome their resistance to change, and offer compelling solutions. We know that on any given day there are countless signed orders that have resulted from those undertakings between buyer and seller.

But I have an axe to grind. I believe that current sales training is flawed in its avoidance of discussing the true nature of the competition we face. It seems that many so-called experts spout rhetoric that would have us believe that the competition is between us and the prospect.

Let's discuss.

The Competition

In all of our coaching and training material we ask people to embrace the following:

> **Every potential customer we meet is comparing the experience they have with us to the various experiences they have with others. Our success in**

selling comes largely from making the other experiences pale by comparison.

We also need to recognize the following three points regarding competition:

- **Competition is always present.**

- **We are always being compared to the competition.**

- **We win sales against our competition by exceeding expectations.**

We have heard that knowing one's competition is a precept of strategy. It's also natural to associate the word "competition" with the direct competition we face in business as in Pepsi versus Coke, Avis versus Hertz, and Your Company versus Her Company. However, by viewing the competition with such a narrow scope, we commit a strategic error. In reality we always compete with our prospective buyers' everyday experiences much more than we compete against our direct trade competition.

Think about that. All of us live in a stream of experiences that are pleasing or displeasing, fulfilling or unfulfilling, mundane or extraordinary, tedious or fun.

If we are competing against a prospect's everyday experiences, we can agree that it constitutes a much broader range than those individuals or companies that we refer to as "my competition."

Is our direct competition important? Of course it is. The task of maintaining knowledge of our competitors is a crucial part of a salesperson's job. It works hand in hand with our accumulation of product knowledge. Such information allows us to establish a unique selling proposition, an identifiable difference. This falls under the heading of preparedness, and we are being asked to completely accept that preparedness is the most important skill in selling.

At this very moment, there's a good chance that somewhere there are individuals who are contemplating buying jet airplanes for their companies. As we might expect, there are men and women who sell jet airplanes. Those airplane buyers live on the same planet we do, so there is a very good chance that many of them have experienced the same kind of happenings that we encounter. Let's take a look at what some of those experiences might be. Of course, I don't buy or sell airplanes, and I don't have a close relationship with anybody that does. However, I can personally attest to the authenticity of the following. Do these experiences ring a bell?

The jet airplane salesperson competes with:

- The important package which is sent late. (A wise man once told me that when we keep people waiting, they spend the time counting our faults.)

- The restaurant owner who insists on charging for an extra slice of tomato.

- The clerks who now say "There you go." instead of "Thank you." or say "No problem." instead of "You're welcome." when we thank them.

- The eye doctor who overbooks appointments and keeps you waiting too long in the waiting room.

- The salesperson that makes every call an intrusion.

- People who do not listen.

- Vendors who don't get back on time with a quotation.

- People who don't return phone calls.

- People who forget to keep their promises.

I guess we should have added people who give us "the finger" in traffic.

Such is life. We get the idea. Those are examples of individuals and companies that are chipping away at the expectation levels of the general population. Obviously it's easy to provide a better experience for people we come across in your daily activities, albeit those that would become our prospective buyers. However, there are loads of people in this world who expect greater things of themselves. And--they are our competition too.

The hard ones, the toughest nuts to crack, are on the march. They are the ones that engage current and prospective customers in a caring and efficient way. For them, it's an ongoing campaign to differentiate themselves from us--their competition. They have not let the expectations of others compromise their belief in themselves or their focus on presenting themselves in the best possible light. They do it through their actions. They are our elite competition. They show up on time, make and keep promises, and follow through with a passion. They not only listen, they hear. They not only hear, they demonstrate that they have heard. They never call without a purpose. They are caring, courteous, and empathetic. They seek conditions of mutual trust and respect with prospective buyers. More often than not, they achieve those conditions. Intentions are powerful.

In our workshops, we coined the term, "Bar of Expectations." The term's use is two-fold. We know that the general buying public has expectations that have been influenced by the good, bad, and indifferent experiences they have had with those whose job it is to serve them. And we know that the superior salesperson practices her craft to surpass her prospects' and clients' expectations. She sets her very own level and she sets it high. Her aspirations become inspirations to those she encounters.

You and I must constantly expect and demand the best of ourselves while delivering the very best to those we engage. That is the real territory we manage.

SEVENTEEN
Getting Feedback Continuously

NOTHING HAS MORE impact in setting a salesperson on the right course than a prospective buyer's feedback. No question could be more important than those we ask a prospect on how he feels about what we have presented at any particular stage of the conversation. Nothing is easier to attain than the answers a prospect would provide us.

Yet, the feedback goes untapped among a vast portion of men and women who sell for a living.

I have never surveyed the reason why so many sales people are reluctant to ask for feedback. I do have my beliefs and they are mostly intuitive. There is a notion that has been going around for years that says we should never ask a question that can be answered with a "no." That is advice that should adorn our wastebasket. If I am showing a particular product or sharing a solution, I want to know what the prospect thinks about it. The truth is I need to know. I make a habit of asking for feedback. I do it with honest questions. I have never gotten a response that was less than valuable by asking honest questions like the following:

- **"Tell me what you're thinking."**

    That's really a command, isn't it? But it's a common way of expressing a query.

- **"Do you like the _____?"**

    There is such power in those five words and we can view them as a test close if we're simply willing to use them.

- **"What's missing?"**

    That's an invitation for a prospect to tell us what her real buying trigger is. It is far superior to asking, "What else would you like to know?" We have to be cautious with that one. We may get a reply like, "Nothing, really. I think you've covered everything." It's often a very polite dismissal. Worse, it implies that the prospect believes she knows all she needs to know. Closing sales is a progression, and it's one where the seller needs to be at the helm.

- **"Does what I've told you make good sense?"**

    Wow! If the answer is "no" you're in trouble. I have never heard that reply. However, we won't get too carried away when we hear the stock reply, "Yes."

GETTING FEEDBACK CONTINUOUSLY

- **"Tell me what comes next."**

    That's another of those polite commands.

- **"Is this compatible with your budget?"**

    Up until the time they sign the order, qualifying never really stops.

- **"In addition to what you've told me, is there any other reason you would not want to move ahead with this now?"**

    That one is still powerful after all these years.

- **"What's your timetable on this project?"**

    That question is often a bridge to the facilitation and softens the transition into finalizing the deal.

- **"What would you like to accomplish?"**

    This is a good question for the prospect who is trying to get the lowest price by beating around the bush or tossing obstacles our way.

Those are time-tested questions that are very effective for gaining information and setting the sales conversation on the right course. I describe those questions as "honest." An honest question is one that we ask because we would like to know the answer. Manipulative questions are those that are asked for the purpose of leading the prospect into a predetermined answer. Manipulative questions are usually very transparent. In our training we teach that honest insightful questions are the building blocks of sales. Rhetorical questions often fall into the manipulative category. Of course they are not really questions; they are statements in disguise. Rhetorical questions are rarely honest. They range from harmless and ineffective to harmful, conniving, and adversarial. I'm well aware that they are common in conversations. It would be extremely difficult to dispense with them completely. So--when I advise not to ask such questions, I'm doing it for two reasons. First, they clutter or pollute the skill sets for effective questioning that a serious salesperson needs to develop. Second, I want to create an awareness that will drastically reduce their use in favor of honest questions.

For a long time I have noticed that the movers and shakers of the world are not afraid to say what they believe as well as ask what they want to know. There is a tendency, in fact, for many of them to preface their statements by saying, "Let me tell you what I believe." On the other hand, people who have an affinity for asking rhetorical questions always seem to be on the losing end of some debate. Worse, I have heard people voice those questions in a way that reveals either sarcasm or passive aggressive behavior.

Shortly after some blurbs about my last book went viral, I got a message on a social networking web site from an author of some sort of book on selling. He began with, *"Why would I want to buy your book when I have a book (name of his book)?"* Needless to say, that conversation never got off the ground. Imagine if I took his question seriously as if it was honest rather than rhetorical. I would have had to engage in a needs analysis for the guy that could run for hours if not days? All to sell a book!

If you don't know, ask. It pays big dividends.

EIGHTEEN
A Very Important Person

GATEKEEPERS!

I know that word comes up in discussions, usually among salespeople who can't get through the receptionist, secretary, administrative assistant, or office manager, so they can meet with the person they would like to talk to. Do you suppose that the individuals who decided to coin the word did it because they were obstructed? The use of the word has also been popularized by sales trainers who appear to have their own problems with getting consent from those people who could facilitate a conversation with a decision maker. Would the label have existed if they were succeeding in their efforts?

I get asked, "How do I get past the gatekeeper?" That's like asking, "How do I sell?" Remember how we talked about how closing is a progression of consent? Well, if we're having trouble getting consent from someone we are labeling as gatekeeper, how are we going to get consent higher up the ladder?

A VERY IMPORTANT PERSON

I don't call people gatekeepers because I don't think we should go around labeling people. It seems to me that it contributes to a wrong mindset. There is no profit in adopting a communication style or attitude born of others' frustration. Isn't it better to adopt a language of people who get results?

Okay, so it's true that part of an employee's role might be perceived as protector of her boss from annoyances and time wasters. It's true they often want to know more about your purpose before they'll budge. No "receptionist" is going to be receptive to fancy sales speak or transparent approaches that serve no purpose other than to intrude. What people are willing to do is offer help when asked for help. It's part of human nature that transcends the protector role. When we talk to these individuals, we can talk to them as one human being to another and we can ask for help. We could even tell them that we might be approaching the wrong person or the wrong department. We can ask, "Could you please point me in the right direction?"

We can ask their names and give them ours. We can smile. We can be super courteous and respectful. It gives people a good feeling to help those who ask for help. It is also normal to disdain transparency. So long as we think of other human beings as "gatekeepers", and label them as such, we won't enlist their support. There's karma in selling as there is in most things in life. When we see those people as obstructive ogres, they will see us as intruders.

Can we get past this person? Why not think of it as engaging a person who can facilitate our audience with a decision maker? It can be a milestone in an important progression of consent.

Okay, here's the best reason of all to embrace the counsel I'm handing out in this chapter. It is very possible that the individual known as a gatekeeper is the second most important person in the whole company!

NINETEEN
Working With Triplicates

THE NUMERAL 3 is the magic number in the art of presentation. Regardless of whether we believe in magic or believe that presentation is an art, let's see if we can make magic and art work in our behalf.

Now that we're exploring that suggestion, I'll practice what I preach. Here are three things to consider:

1. We can't overestimate our prospect's attention span. Not only is she evaluating our message; she's evaluating us. Our job is to get three important pieces of information across. Once again, it's quality, not quantity, that counts.
2. Preparedness is the most important skill in selling. Every contact we make with a prospective buyer should be a purposeful call (no exceptions). When we prepare three meaningful points to discuss, we come across in an organized and professional manner. It invites conversation and participation.

WORKING WITH TRIPLICATES

3. Preparing three areas of discussion is easy. Trying to cover too many areas in one conversation will dilute our effectiveness and make it difficult for our prospect to provide valuable feedback.

The triplicate model surfaces often in selling. The "ready, willing, able" standard of qualifying a prospect is an example. Note the three questions in that standard assessment:

1. Is he ready to buy?
2. Is he willing to buy?
3. Is he able to buy?

How about the classic advice on presentation?

1. Tell them what you're going to tell them.
2. Tell it to them.
3. Tell them what you told them.

There were no less than fifty six signers of The Declaration of Independence and we do know what they say about committees. Those Founding Fathers arrived at agreement on one of the most important documents in human history by focusing on three central ideas. They were: Life, Liberty, and, The Pursuit of Happiness.

It's no coincidence that I just gave three examples.

What is often described in such a sterile manner as a sales "process" is really a sales conversation from start to finish. In many selling situations, it could take place in one sitting. In others, depending on the nature of the industry, it could be extended over days, weeks, or longer. Each and every contact we make should demonstrate a purpose whether it is for gathering information, or for conveying ideas about solutions. Purposeful activity enhances the leadership role of the salesperson. Working with triplicates organizes and structures our communication in an impressive manner and makes it easier to assume the leadership role. Many novices in selling have not come to the realization that most buyers like to be led. Top performers have accepted the fact.

To summarize, the simple message here is to structure every contact you have with a prospect so that you get three issues covered. That is preparedness which, once again, is the most important skill in selling.

TWENTY
The Artists Aren't Starving

IN THE MID-NINETIES, the Internet was still in a lagging infancy stage. The majority of small to mid-sized companies and organizations were still without any meaningful Web presence. Blogging had not become a household word. The various search engines had not been rubbed out by a few innovators that would become dominant and all powerful. There were ideas about how to make big money on the web, but they had not crossed the threshold from mind to matter. Some of us were still grinning at funny names like Yahoo and Google. Online auctions and booksellers had not gained status as a way of life. There were forums and chat rooms but they were mostly esoteric. Porn was emerging as the biggest online industry. Search engine optimization was so simple you could learn it in a four hour class along with a primer thrown in on HTML. I know--I took such a class. Ask me about SEO now and I'll tell you I'm running late for an appointment.

So who would have ever thought?

In those days, web sites were thought of as a commodity. They were a monitor screen you could advertise on. That was before the word "advertise" became tainted in favor of "market" perhaps because of the high costs and risky returns associated with advertising. Many companies started taking the plunge onto the net with "brochure sites" to get their message across. It was an apt description because the content contained little more than what you would find on a tri-fold printed brochure. Not many sites were interactive, and people were still very reserved about putting credit card information onto the few shopping carts that did exist.

I got involved when a building trade organization asked me to give a talk to their members about the Internet. I saw it as an opportunity to ply my skills in sales and advertising if some of the members would take me on as a paid consultant to facilitate a web presence. Surprisingly, with the first talk I gave, I hit pay dirt. Three members paid me an advance and I immediately became a dime store guru.

In my talk, I said two things which resonated with the group. My magic words came towards the end of my talk and I admit they were not impromptu. I had rehearsed them. I knew then what I know now; preparedness is the most important skill in selling.

I said to the group, "The Internet will become a powerful tool and like all powerful tools it will be more powerful if you know its limitations." I then said, "Everybody who's aware of this Internet thing seems to want to know where it's all going. The fact is I don't think anybody knows. But that's not a good enough answer to leave you with tonight. So I'll offer you something better.

As far as each one of you is concerned, the Internet is going to exactly where you want to take it."

I had the three people who gave me advances rolling in the aisles.

The Connection Economy

Seth Godin, a man I consider to be the best business author around, says that we now live in the connection economy. I agree. He says we need to be artists at this time in history. I agree. It is the artists that are connecting regardless of how they make their way in the world.

Anthony Robbins has said that the quality of our lives depends on the quality of our communication. Technology is giving us more ways to communicate every day. Are we communicating better? It took millions of years to get from Neanderthal man to today's homo sapiens model. Along the way and for thousands of years we have had great thinkers and communicators that would put us to shame. I see hordes of people tapping on their iPhones while sitting across from their dinner companions. I have too much empathy in me to believe they are inherently rude. I have no first stones to cast. We have let technology grab us by the ear.

We hear a lot of talk about courage and the need for it to manifest in our sales careers. It seems the talk is always about overcoming the fear of rejection. Sometimes we hear about fear of success. "Call reluctance" is a term that appeared on the scene a few years ago. I am not reluctant to express my views on the subject. I have no fear of rejection if you disagree with what I am about to say. I have no fear of being successful in getting my point across to you.

The Courage to Express

The courage we need to manifest in our careers is the same courage we need to carry in life. We need to, without surrendering to fear, express our beliefs, express our beings, express our real concerns, express our love, express our passion, and express what we want to accomplish. Whatever tools or whatever technology we have, today or in the future, we must not allow them to sabotage our need to express because what we express defines our place in the world. Those tools, now and in the unknown future, will matter only if we use them to open ourselves up to others.

Are we using social media to market ourselves or our company or our products? Are we creating a good experience for those who connect with us? Are we asking honest questions because we have prepared ourselves to do so? Are we making progress?

Sound bites don't build relationships anymore than they reflect the truth. How do we want to express ourselves using today's technology? Do we want to type four letter acronyms to tell people we're rolling on the floor laughing? Do we really think that the texting language of little symbols really makes people think we're smiling when we could express, "You make me smile." just as easily?

If this sounds touchy feely, I invite the reader to rethink it. In a world that provides more ways to connect than in any time in history, a lot of us are failing to connect. On sites like Facebook, a lot of people are using it to preach their delusions or tell the world what their hamster ate for dinner. Wastelands only become wastelands when they become barren of substance.

As much as we plan and try to project the future, the good stuff that happens to us will come out of the void--the great unknown. In my opinion, that's the number one reason why we need to take the ever-increasing tools for connecting and start using them to connect meaningfully.

The artist who lives inside you or lives inside me can do that.

EPILOGUE

I WOULD NEVER be as foolish as to attempt to write an all-inclusive treatise on the subject of selling. Opportunities in this profession come in too many flavors and nothing can be described as "all relevant" more than the flighty thing we sometimes call success. To once again paraphrase Stephen Covey, I have sought to understand, and then to be understood. I believe that without those words, the Four Applied Understandings for Success in Selling would still be on the launching pad.

If selling for a living makes you happy, I suspect you're doing a lot of things right. If you're not quite there, and you sometimes wonder why, I'll offer some bona fide career advice. Please always remember to periodically ask yourself this question:

***Am I the right person selling the
right product for the right reasons?***

Somewhere in the future as we make our way in the world, I hope to meet up with you again. Whether it is on the road, or competing with one another, or in the pages of my

EPILOGUE

next effort, I want us to learn from one another. Until such time I want you to know....

I really do appreciate you.

Gary Boye

May of 2014

APPENDIX

AUTHOR'S NOTE:
I compiled questions for this section that originate from composites of questions that surfaced in discussions, courses, and forums regarding material presented in this book. In addition, I also took the liberty of creating questions that would afford me an opportunity to inject a few further insights on the individual topics. For purely selfish reasons, I invite other questions from readers. You can submit them to *garyboye3@gmail.com*. I will make an effort to reply and I will take them into consideration for future entries in our Sales Mastery Series. Also, any future revisions of this text will reflect current readers' requests for clarification.

> **Q: The book points out immediately a belief that there are four and only four understandings that determine our success in selling? Isn't that presumptuous? Isn't selling a field that requires a much more comprehensive model than that?**

APPENDIX

A: First of all, "model" is definitely the right word. The Four Applied Understandings are presented as a model through which we can filter and discern all other factors and ideas regardless of how broad we want to go in our methodologies. They don't represent a limit to what we must learn. Instead they represent a gateway unto meaningful knowledge as they guard us from what is not meaningful. A lot of people call selling a science. If it is, we need scientists. I practice selling as an art. I have used the scientist's habit of keen observation and testing long before I had the audacity to express my thoughts on the matter. There is nothing elitist about it. I think some of the best auto mechanics are scientists of a sort. They go in and they fiddle around and decide what works and what doesn't.

Q: Throughout these pages, you keep referring to honest questions. Aren't most questions in selling manipulative? Aren't we supposed to control with questions?

A: When I refer to honest questions, I often add the word, "insightful," to further describe them. Many salespeople ask manipulative questions. Many sales trainers and books teach their use. So--the answer to the first question is yes. My attitude toward this is reflected in the introduction to this book. I tried to remain consistent with that attitude throughout. Questions are for gaining information which can, in turn, forward the conversation.

APPENDIX

Q: You said closing is not an event; it is a progression. If I ask for a decision, such as asking for the order, isn't that an event?

A: Yes. But it's not a close. It's a closing question. And I would hope it's an honest one. We need to be at the point in the progression where it's appropriate.

Q: How can preparedness be called the most important skill in selling?

A: For one, it defines us as professionals. The term "sales professional" has not been around forever. If we're going to adopt it, there has to be standards. We would expect a heart surgeon to be prepared also.

Q: You mentioned that extraordinary salespeople prepare for the expected. It would be easier to believe the opposite which is preparing for the unexpected. Can you clarify?

A: The things that we come to expect are derived from past experiences. In sales, it's our job to find remedies for issues that we experience and expect to face again. If we're facing the same stances of resistance from our prospects on a daily basis, it certainly would pay to be prepared with ways to transcend those stances. I wanted to make that point in the book because I have seen too many salespeople falter on the same obstacles over and over without preparing a solution.

Q: Hasn't the sales model known by the acronym **AIDCA** recently been modified? Now we hear of **AIDAS** which stands for attention, interest, desire, action, and satisfaction. The

APPENDIX

theory is that after the buyer has bought the product, you need to reassure him that he has made the right decision.

A: That's not the first time AIDCA has been modified. In AIDA, for instance, the conviction step was deleted. But AIDAS, which has a post sale satisfaction step, has reinvented what I described as a flawed model by adding another flaw. Meeting conditions of satisfaction (in the agreement) has to take place before the final agreement is reached. Delivering on those promises of satisfaction is another matter that is contained elsewhere in the relationship between seller and customer. The marketing of service is in the service. Notice how that simple statement aligns with the first of The Four Applied Understandings.

Q: It's been said that closing a sale consists of a series of minor agreements that culminate in a final and conclusive major agreement. Is that the same as saying that closing is a progression of consent?

A: It's a working model and it has been formulated many times by direct sales organizations. In some cases, the steps were scripted as questions, usually in conjunction with "assumed closes." That method has a history of some success. However, the model fails to recognize that the major agreement or consent often happens way before the agreement that represents a purchase. When we view closing as a progression of consent, we don't hardwire in advance where the major decision will take place.

APPENDIX

Q: In Chapter Eight you characterized the categories of resistance as "perceived." Why?

A: It's impossible to know exactly what's in a prospect's mind or what he is feeling during a conversation. What we bring back from a sales call is our own perception. The closer you can come to knowing the real reasons that a prospect is resisting, the greater the chance for a sale.

Q: Why does the chapter on buyer resistance reflect a negative view of the use of the word "objection?"

A: Yes, I have had a problem with that word. It always seemed that we were supposed to believe that objections in a sales engagement come about in orderly fashion, and we are to "handle" them with swiftness, or grace, or provocation, and ride smoothly into a signed order. In all my years, I did not see it happen that way very often. But I did enjoy many smooth rides from start to finish. There's a difference, and it lies in seeing the whole picture. The topic is "resistance" and it could be referred to as the clay we have to mold a sale from. Either that, or, walk away--which we are not yet ready to do. Resistance is there, and, it exists as inertia that wants things to stay in place. It certainly is the core challenge in the practice of selling.

Q: You mentioned the "one call close." Has selling advanced beyond that?

A: Not at all. The reason I differentiate is that I

APPENDIX

take issue with a lot of sales training material that ignores the length of a selling cycle completely.

Q: We hear a lot about "added value" offers. Do they fall under the heading of unique selling propositions, emotional Selling propositions, or obvious Selling Propositions?

A: It could be any or all of the above. The term, "added value", often confuses people for some reason. I did not use it in this book. Perhaps a better term would be "sweetening the pot." It will make for a whole chapter in another book in this series.

Q: Isn't the use of the word "clueless" unkind when the book describes an early stage in a selling career?

A: Yes, I agree. However, I am expressing my disdain for a system that does not adequately provide training. The newcomers are those who I have much empathy for. My memory is not that short.

Q: Were you serious in stating that the person being labeled a gatekeeper might often be the second most powerful person in the company?

A: Yes, if not the most powerful!

Q: Are many or all of today's new tools for communicating undermining our abilities to connect meaningfully?

APPENDIX

A: No. As individuals we still have a choice. The message in Chapter Twenty is really a call for people to choose to connect by expressing themselves more openly.

Q: Where will we go from here with The Sales Mastery Series?

A: Stay tuned.

ABOUT THE AUTHOR

Gary Boye is an American sales strategist who, along with master practitioner Jeff Blackwell, presides over the ongoing development of the *Sales Education Alliance*, a consultancy designed for serious professionals. As an adviser on sales related issues, companies and individuals retain his services for addressing critical challenges and difficult marketing projects.

Gary has been a mentor and coach in various sales arenas, including financial planning, insurance, textiles, dental marketing, automotive, and building trades. His direct response marketing campaigns have been modeled by several companies. He has led seminars on strategy in the United States and Canada, and served on the advisory panels of three multinational companies. He is the recipient of several national sales contest first place awards.

In 2011, Jeff and Gary formed the *Sales Education Alliance* to collaborate on training and education related projects. Gary's *Twice as Good as 2nd Best*™ and Jeff's *SalesPractice*™ brands of professional and management

ABOUT THE AUTHOR

development training are made available through the Sales Education Alliance. Together, they have created The *SalesPractice Certification Program* with the intention of bringing accreditation to sales professionals who meet standards of applied understanding and skills.

His second entry in the Sales Mastery Series, Tough Love for Easy Selling is available on Amazon Kindle.

Gary enjoys playing four wall handball and sailing his small sloop, Little Orca, in beautiful Lake Chautauqua. He joins friends at Seven Seas Sailing on Lake Erie where he directs the wine tasting on Friday nights. Stop by for a sail and a sip. He lives outside of Buffalo, NY.

Gary is always accessible to serious people. He can be reached at **716-799-5655** or at **garyboye@gmail.com**.

www.ingramcontent.com/pod-product-compliance
Lightning Source LLC
Chambersburg PA
CBHW051808170526
45167CB00005B/1928